Exporters!

The Wit and Wisdom of Small Businesspeople Who Sell Globally

Doug Barry
U.S. Commercial Service Global Knowledge Center

U.S. Commercial Service—Connecting you to global markets.

Table of Contents

Introduction

This book is an effort to share with you the stories of ordinary folks doing extraordinary things, making products and performing services for customers throughout the world. Most of the companies are very small, with fewer than 10 employees, and many started in one of the familiar business incubators: a basement, a garage, or a kitchen.

What is unusual about the stories is their scarcity. Out of the millions of U.S. businesses, only about 1.5 percent, or about 300,000 individual companies, made an international sale in 2012. Over half of those companies exported to only one market. Of all industrialized countries, the U.S. is third to last in the percentage of gross domestic product (GDP) generated by exports. This book features 28 of these stories, drawn with permission and without specific selection criteria from the active client files of the U.S. Commercial Service, the trade promotion organization of the U.S. Commerce Department, and supported by interviews with principals of the companies selected.

The purpose of the book is to demystify the act of selling a good or service to a buyer in another country. In sharing these stories, we go beyond a simple, "They did it, so you can do it, too," perspective. Instead, we let the exporters themselves explain how they did it, assuming that many of the lessons learned are applicable to others and can be successfully employed by you if you choose to follow a similar path.

Before presenting these mini-oral histories of exporters and their exporting companies, we first provide some context and then identify themes derived from the stories.

Exporting and Domestic Economic Policy

In 2012, U.S. exports of goods and services topped a record $3 trillion, further cementing the nation's position as the world's number one exporter. As noted, though not necessarily as a positive, in that year about 300,000 U.S. companies, most of them small or midsized, exported a tangible product or service. That is the highest number since the government started keeping records.

In 2011, the U.S. lost its number one position as the world's top manufacturer when China surged into the lead. The U.S. remains the number one exporter of services and thus in combined manufactures and services. And, of course, many of China's manufacturing exports consist of U.S. intellectual property, with the majority of the value accruing to U.S. patent holders.

If the U.S. is number one, why is this book in part celebrating the importance of small-size companies and encouraging readers to join them? The reasons include:

- the current trillions of dollars are good for the economy and still more cash is needed;
- exporting companies create higher paying jobs, putting the unemployed to work and contributing to federal and local government tax bases;
- many more companies could export but don't;
- products not now exported by U.S. companies can contribute to the quality of life of people living outside the U.S. and to the solution of important environmental and other global problems;
- new companies starting up every day need international sales to survive and to grow;
- of the existing active U.S. exporting companies, 58 percent sell to only one market, most typically Canada;

- the experience of adapting products and services for sale to non-U.S. markets contributes to the national storehouse of knowledge and to personal and professional growth in a world that is increasingly interconnected and competitive; and

- the broad benefits generated by exporting and exporters is not only a private good, it is also a public good.

Given the benefits of encouraging more exports and exporters, it's no surprise that there's rare bipartisan support for export promotion public policy. One example is the Obama administration's National Export Initiative (NEI), which seeks to double the value of exports and create millions of jobs over five years. U.S. exports were up by double digits for the first two years, 2011 and 2012. Meanwhile, global growth has encountered headwinds, and it's unclear where things will stand in 2015 when the NEI ends. However, achieving dollar public policy goals is not as important as meeting the need to build and sustain public awareness and interest in the broad benefits of exporting. This book aims to contribute to this awareness building, while seeking to tell a compelling story within a familiar genre—the small-business success narrative.

We preface the stories with some introductory points: the context for judging the importance of what the exporting companies do; why there aren't more of them; who they are; and what appear to be key reasons for their success.

Familiar Genre, Rare Stories

My colleagues and I have worked for many years with people and their companies like the ones featured here. We find their stories endlessly fascinating, instructive, even uplifting. One of the reasons to share more widely what they've done is the relative rareness of such successes. Out of over 2 million businesses in the U.S., only a small portion sell outside the country—thus engaging in the process called exporting.

Since the boom in world trade beginning after World War II, exporting from the U.S. by value has been dominated by large companies—defined as those with more than 500 employees and with substantial annual revenues. Though this dominance continues, the number of small companies exporting has been slowly increasing, as has the total value of what they sell. Also headed higher is the value of U.S. exports.

When the 2012 data are finalized, the number of U.S. companies exporting something of value will reach a record of more than 300,000; of these, 98 percent are small and midsize firms.

While still only a mere 1.5 percent of all U.S. companies, many of which are neighborhood shops unlikely to export anything soon, the number of businesses joining the export market has risen steadily over the last 20 years. In 1992 there were 108,000 exporters. Then during the next 8 years the number more than doubled to around 238,000 in 2000. The number of companies exporting continued to rise, reaching more than 282,000 in 2008, before sliding back to 270,000 in 2009, the bottom of the worldwide recession. That only 12,000 fewer companies exported that year is a sign of the durability of the trend and of the companies that have embraced exporting as a survival strategy, if not a path to growth.

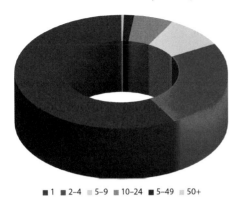

Number of Markets Served by U.S. Exporters

■ 1 ■ 2–4 ■ 5–9 ■ 10–24 ■ 5–49 ■ 50+

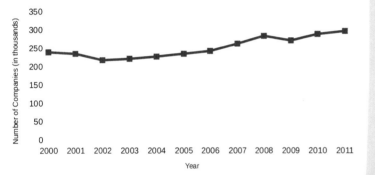

Number of Identified U.S. Small and Medium-Sized Enterprises Exporting

Number of Companies (in thousands)

350
300
250
200
150
100
50
0

2000 2001 2002 2003 2004 2005 2006 2007 2008 2009 2010 2011

Year

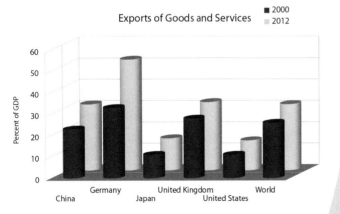

Exports of Goods and Services

■ 2000
■ 2012

Percent of GDP

60
50
40
30
20
10
0

China   Germany   Japan   United Kingdom   United States   World

The year 2010 signaled recovery, with 286,661 companies exporting, a record to that point. Still, year-over-year growth in the number of individual companies exporting is not making anyone watery eyed. For 2011, it will probably be 5 percent more than 2010 or about 7,000 companies. That's worth applauding, but there are many more companies that could be selling to the 98 percent of the world's consumers who live outside the U.S.

While the number of exporting companies has increased, the number of countries they sell to has not. Over the many years such data have been collected, 58 percent of U.S. companies export to precisely . . . one market. And that market is mainly Canada. Imagine the impact if more than half of the country's exporters were able to double the number of export markets to . . . two markets.

A much smaller group of exporters sell to multiple markets, but this group is typical of the exporters profiled in the book. For example, the percentage of companies exporting to between 10 and 24 different countries increased from 4.8 percent of exporters in 2001 to 5.9 percent in 2010. The reasons company A sells to only one market, while company B sells to 50, are unclear. From the conversations with dozens of exporters that resulted in this book, some plausible explanations and factors emerge—and are discussed in detail later in this section.

As an exporting nation, the U.S. is underperforming, and not only by the measure of the number of companies that have figured out how to do it profitably. Another more popular and probably more revealing measure is the percentage of GDP contributed by exports. In the

U.S., it's about **14 percent** of the total output of goods and services. In **Germany** it's closer to 50 percent. Japan's exports contribute about 12 percent of GDP, considerably less than in previous years, because many Japanese manufacturers have moved production offshore to other countries, including the U.S. Closer to home, **Canada's exports contribute about 40 percent** of GDP. At the other extreme, **Ireland's exports contribute almost 98 percent of GDP.**

As one wit said, the world must be drinking a lot of Guinness beer. But this isn't quite right. Multinational computer chip vendors, drug makers, and others account for most of the exports. Local companies export much less, and it's these companies the Irish government, like governments elsewhere, including the U.S., are trying to encourage to export more. This is not to say that it's always better to have more of GDP depend on exports. Analysts have begun warning that Germany's export-dependent economy is slowing with little in the way of domestic demand to take up the slack. By this measure, Ireland is even more vulnerable.

But as the world's factories get going again, countries can look for the right balance, including the optimal GDP and numbers of companies exporting. **If the U.S. could pull policy levers to double the percentage of GDP generated by exports, millions of new jobs would be created.**

What kinds of public policy can help bring this about, not just for the U.S. but for other countries as well? The U.S. is currently doing many of the right things. Focusing on the importance of the economic benefits of exporting is a good start.

Making it easier for companies to export is an important part of the mix. Government-funded export education programs and export loan guarantees are near the top of policy prescriptions. So, too, is making sure other countries and companies play by the rules. Regional free-trade agreements, which reduce duties and make doing business easier, increase trade and the number of companies engaging in it. Immigration policies that encourage investors with a passion for trading increase the pool of expertise that countries wanting to increase exports need. A quality education system is a must to fill the pipeline with young people who enjoy making things and to train those who will work for them.

About the Author

Doug Barry is a senior trade specialist with the U.S. Commercial Service. His previous books include *A Basic Guide to Exporting* (10th edition) and *Free Trade Agreements: 20 Ways to Grow Your Business*. He grew up in the San Francisco area, taught at the University of Alaska, and received a doctorate from Columbia University in New York City. He lives in Washington, DC, with his wife and youngest daughter. He is grateful to his colleagues in the Global Knowledge Center, especially Gary Bouck for the careful editing of the manuscript and to his bosses, Susan Lusi, Tom McGinty, Anand Basu, and Antwaun Griffin for supporting the project.

Most of all he wishes to thank those who made this book possible: all the exporters who shared their inspiring stories, talking frankly about their successes and shortcomings. Thanks in part to their efforts, exporting by small businesses will one day cease to be an unusual event performed by a relatively few people. Instead, it will simply be—business.

Themes and Lessons

Exporting Has Been Key to Growth and, in Some Cases, Survival

The companies featured in this book have grown—spectacularly in a number of cases—by selling their goods and services outside North America. Unlike the majority of small-business exporters, the folks featured here operate businesses that sell to markets in multiple countries. One exporter, who sells to customers in more than a hundred countries, described his position like this: "At this point, international revenue is about 75 percent of our business. We have thousands of active resale channels in about 125 countries. We are a micro-multinational."

Others credit exporting with saving the entire company during a major downturn in the U.S. market: "Truly speaking, during the recession in 2008 when everything kind of collapsed, I looked at all my rigs parked, and said, 'What am I going to do with this?' Going international became a matter of necessity, not just a whim. And I said, 'We have to look at an international way to survive.'"

"Last year we sold $63 million in products and services to customers in 60 countries."

Another company sees its exporting activities in a larger context, as a kind of exporting ecosystem: "Our international business is about 15 percent of our revenue. And that's 15 percent from almost nothing. You can imagine, with that kind of momentum, that's becoming a bigger part of our business every year. We're hiring people. We're keeping other people employed, not just in our company, but other people working with trucking, logistics, banking, letters of credit, packaging; all kinds of people are working because we are shipping containers of stuff."

A service company executive also mentioned dramatic growth in international sales and the excitement of adding new workers: "There are 40 of us at headquarters, and we expect to add 30 more next year. Revenues hit $1 billion in 2011. The company's international success has contributed to our growth."

Another company owner said, "Last year about 50 percent of our business was international. This year it may be even greater." And a young business owner in California said, "Last year we sold $63 million in products and services to customers in 60 countries."

Rich Learning: Exporting Generates Better Companies and Better Products and Services

For many of the people featured in the book, the number one benefit of exporting is what they learn from their customers. The learning, which takes place on different levels, can be categorized as learning about the technical aspects of selling a product or service to a buyer in another country; learning that contributes to improvements in the product or services and business processes; and learning that enhances the capabilities of the business owner or officer—namely in sales, marketing, strategic planning, and managing relationships. None of this comes as a major surprise, since it appears in academic literature, but these points may not be widely appreciated by the larger business public. The people directly benefiting from this learning must be inclined to recognize it as valuable and to apply its lessons for tangible, measurable results. Of course, not all U.S. exporters do, and some holdouts nevertheless achieve a level of success. But those who are mindful about their learning have a different story to tell.

One business owner, reflecting on the benefit of an intercultural experience, had this to say: "I think it's the fear barrier, right? It's confidence and the ability to take on something that you're not sure of—probably similar to what you learn in terms of engineering skills and attacking a new problem. Engineers that I've dealt with over my career are rather insular and have relatively few business capabilities coming out of school. And pushing them into an international business experience is a quick way to go from zero to 100 miles an hour. And every aspect of the trip [to Korea] and the relationships and the expectations and the cultural norms are different and challenge the engineers to get out of their established ways."

The international sales manager for a large building equipment manufacturer described the transformative potential of getting out of one's "established ways": "The experience in international markets has made me a more effective professional and the company more competitive in every market we serve, including the U.S. We simplified our product right down to our software so everything is easier to operate, no matter what the physical conditions or the language spoken. Our key personnel have grown from the international experience, and we continuously bring ideas back home and apply them throughout the company."

An international sales manager for a medical equipment company leaves on each trip abroad with the assumption that she will learn something new and useful. "I feel like our being a global company is giving us a competitive advantage over companies in the same industry that are not present internationally. When you're present and mindful, you see things going on there that are precursors to trends that will eventually come to the U.S. I take a lot of pictures with my smartphone, and people in my company rely on me to send a text or photo. 'Hey, I'm at this hospital; look at what I'm seeing? Isn't that interesting?' And I'll shoot that over and people will take a look and say, 'Huh, well that is interesting.' So it's definitely allowing us to be a better company and to have a competitive edge."

> **For many of the people featured in this book, the number one benefit of exporting is what they learn from their customers.**

Here's a final example in this category. The owner of a small technology company has learned to expect, and also to encourage, his international customers to seek new niche markets for his product that he could never anticipate just sitting in his office selling in the North American market. "What we've learned is that everything is both regional and timing, so that something we've done successfully here can be conveyed to another region of the world and they [customers] can replicate that to their clients' benefit, or vice versa. A client overseas may be finding a niche for the technology, having employed it with great success, and then bring that to other segments around the world. So we're learning the interchangeability of success and best practices."

Exporting Companies Are Good at Business Fundamentals

Many of the products and services produced by the exporters in the book are not what you'd classify as unique, though without question the products are well made and the services professionally delivered. For example, there's no apparent shortage of pet care products in the world, including those targeted in the more upscale show dog market. There are a lot of exercise and health equipment manufacturers, but for whatever reason many don't export, or don't see it as a priority. Vitamin supplement makers are plentiful in California and elsewhere in the U.S., but some are still able to find success in the global marketplace despite their number, and because of pricing strategies or good customer service and marketing. There are plenty of elder care companies, but fewer that work hard to become "thought leaders" in the industry.

In the case of successful exporters whose output is not unique, we have to look elsewhere to find the "secret sauce." And in many cases it boils down to "Just get out there." Generate prospects and relentlessly pursue them. One company owner put it this way: "We get the business because we are unafraid to go to places others may overlook or reject."

Many of the people interviewed, each in their own way, marveled over the size of the opportunities seen in the larger world. According to one, "There's plenty of business out there. It's just waiting for us to go get it." Others said that they create opportunities for themselves by offering in their industry what others don't: personal service. As one executive explains: "Customers appreciate how they're able to deal with the owner of the company. And that would be my husband and I."

In relation to access to decision makers, another successful exporter and business owner said, "Warm business is having someone [buyers] can contact that they know is going to help them—to back them up. When we find an overseas buyer, I welcome them into the family. "

The owner of another family business said, "I follow the Three P's: Passion, Perseverance, and Patience. In other words, follow your dream, don't take 'no' for answer, be patient and tackle one problem at a time. You should always ask for assistance and advice when engaging in international business. Don't try to do it alone."

The owner of a small manufacturing company with customers in more than 40 countries focuses on product quality, as do others featured in the book: "We made a conscious business decision that we're going to produce the very best product in the world. Another way to say that is: We don't make junk. And through that, our business reputation over the last several years has grown from when nobody wanted to deal with us to the point where now, on a daily basis, we have incoming requests for quotations from all over the world."

Most of the people interviewed agreed that if you have the desire to sell internationally, and a good product, you can be successful: "If you want to expand globally, you can make this happen. It's just a matter of willpower. If you have a competitive product in this country, you can be competitive overseas. The owner of an environmental service company presented a variation on the quality theme and how it helps to compete successfully in what he described as a global market: "We've had validation of our ideas and, basically, the operating mission of our company, which is its execution. You can't fake it. So if you're going to be in a country and executing in that country, you need to go ready to do the job and do it right."

This does not mean that everyone succeeds. Of 40-plus companies interviewed and followed for more than 6 years, two went bankrupt after a long period of success. It's unclear whether exporting, unfavorable domestic market conditions, or a specific business error led to these failures. The demise of one of the firms, a maker of solar energy products, was caused by weak global demand, oversupply, competition, and plunging prices. Even what seemed at the time to be a smart joint venture with a Chinese partner was not enough to offset these powerful and probably uncontrollable forces. In another instance, an investment in India soured, and the company owner later said that the cause was bad luck and perhaps some business judgments that in retrospect he believes he should have made differently. More convincingly, most of the exporters in the book attribute exporting to their growth. Several said exporting was the key to survival during the dramatic domestic economic downturn of 2008 and 2009.

"And every aspect of the trip [to Korea] and the relationships and the expectations and the cultural norms are different and challenge the engineers to get out of their established ways."

A Belief That the World Is Flat and Competition Should Be Embraced

Many of the people in this book came to the realization that 95 percent of the world's consumers live outside the U.S. This realization was seeded by internationally minded parents in some cases, by travel abroad, and by the individuals' own research. It's now an article of faith as well as a product of direct experience. These businesspeople know they are a minority, and some of them didn't mince words when speaking about the nature of our insularity.

One exporter was especially candid: "The mentality of Americans is to be satisfied with the North American market. That's just plain shortsighted. Their [foreign] competitors in other markets are making money, and sooner or later they'll be here, more competitive because of their experience in some of these developing markets. We're not there. The Chinese are there. We're sitting in North America wondering, 'Is it safe over there?'"

Fear seems to be the number one reason for remaining on the geographical and psychological sidelines. Said one business owner: "The biggest thing that keeps people from entering new markets and new spaces is fear. Fear of the unknown. What I can say is that people are people everywhere I go, that it's really enjoyable to get to know people in other markets. They have families and kids, too, and they're trying to make money. They have a lot of the same motivations. It's very easy to get along with people once you start talking the language of commerce."

Another exporter agreed: "Don't fear the world. The market is huge. If you have a product that's solid and selling in the U.S., there's a good chance that you can compete—at least in some parts of the world. It may be a very necessary step you take for your own survival as well as your growth. So have no fear, and enjoy the great cultural experiences that come with that."

A second big reason for not exporting, according to the literature, is the alleged confounding complexity of the export process—head-snapping regulations, perilous paperwork, and beady-eyed bureaucrats waiting to pounce. Our exporters rejected that reasoning: "We've completely gotten over the overseas part of business as being more difficult than the domestic part; in fact, it's probably now easier for us to grow because the markets are expanding much quicker."

Some exporters love doing it because it's an extension of what they like to do in the U.S.— meet interesting people. "Exporting has changed my life. I love exporting because it has enabled me to meet so many people from other cultures. Exporting has made me more broad minded, and I have developed a great appreciation of other cultures and the way others live their lives. You are put in contact with real people on the other side."

"You should always ask for assistance and advice when engaging in international business. Don't try to do it alone."

Finally, don't be afraid of competition, embrace it, and the experience will make you better. "Competition is tough in these developing markets, but that's where the opportunities are. Exporting is no longer an option, and America's future lies in these markets."

Manufacturing: Advantage U.S.

Most of the manufacturing companies whose executives were interviewed for the book make their products in the U.S. A number of the companies previously manufactured them in other countries, mainly China, but elected for cost, quality control, and other reasons to re-shore, or bring the manufacturing back to the U.S. These companies, then, are not typical, and many U.S. manufacturers will continue to need to make their products in or near the larger markets they serve. But as U.S. companies study cost comparisons and measure the impact of other factors, more will find it advantageous to make things here.

"Manufacturing, back 15 years ago, accounted for . . . I think it was in the area of 36 percent of gross domestic product," said one profiled exporter. "And today, it's down around 18 percent, I think. And the problem with that is that those are the real valuable jobs. It's where you take something, you take an idea and some raw materials, and you convert it into a product. We want to do that in the U.S. and we have to take that technology to the rest of the world."

Another reason these exporters say we'll likely see more manufacturing returning to the U.S. is that consumers have high regard for U.S. products, design, and service and, if necessary, will actually pay more to have the products made in the U.S. All the manufacturing companies featured in the book agreed with this assertion. "The U.S. brand does have cachet. It's related to the expertise, the experience, the technologies. I think many of the purchase decisions [of our international customers] are made based on the fact that what we are bringing to our customers is quite a valued proposition."

Another exporter chimed in with this observation: "Our distributors and customers overseas greatly respect the [environmental] regulation that we've had over the years that's improved our air and water. And 'Made in America' or designed in America or serviced by Americans in many of these countries has a very strong, powerful connotation."

This manufacturer believes that making things in the U.S. holds great future opportunities: "I can tell you from my experience that the U.S. has a brand recognition around the world as being a quality manufacturing location, and so U.S. products are very well received around the world. We have a competitive advantage just because of our brand recognition. So there's huge opportunity there."

Another manufacturer re-shored because he needed more control over the process: "We were running into difficulties in communication about production runs. We pulled [the manufacturing] back and we now have U.S. manufacturers producing our product in small, quick-run quantities. So I see it as a real success story, in general, of what has forced people going offshore, but then bringing it back to the U.S. So we're real happy with it."

The Immigrant Myth That Isn't

Forty-seven percent of startups in tech-heavy Silicon Valley are headed by foreign-born entrepreneurs. The number is actually down from 53 percent in 2010, according to the Kauffman Foundation, a research nonprofit organization that studies entrepreneurship. That announcement briefly perked up interest in immigration reform and had people asking whether there exist sufficient processes and incentives to supplement native-born talent with that from elsewhere. This is an issue that won't, and shouldn't, go away. Meanwhile, people from other countries continue to arrive here and to make their mark, as they have since colonial times. Several of the more recent arrivals are featured in the book, and it's not an exaggeration to summarize their stories as homage to the immigrant myth of hard work, second chances, and bountiful opportunities for people who seize them. What's more, they display both ability to navigate different cultures and fearlessness when it comes to going where the opportunities are.

One of those featured here had this to say: "We're a family-owned business and really have the American story, which is: both Mukund and I were immigrants. We came to this country with very little but lots of big dreams. We wanted to reinvent ourselves, and we want to be the best we can be so that we are able to export U.S. products overseas that are quality and really a win-win for the countries we are doing business with."

Jimmy Wu summed up his story this way: "It has been more than 30 years since my parents overcame hardship in China to bring our family to the U.S. Looking back, I'm so happy to have realized the dream of becoming an American and running an internationally successful business. In fact, I'm living the American dream every day—and enjoying every second."

Willingness to Engage Government Export Assistance Programs

The exporters expressed an overwhelming willingness to work with government agencies at the national and local level. Related to this may be a connection between working with such government programs and the number of markets that the government services users are in. As noted earlier, 58 percent of the 300,000-plus U.S. exporters in 2012 exported to a single market, mostly to Canada. The average number of markets represented by the companies featured in this book is 43. Since the most frequently mentioned solution for these companies is government business matchmaking services—connecting a foreign buyer with a U.S. producer—it seems reasonable to assume that government export promotion services played a role in helping the companies go well beyond a single export market.

According to this manufacturer, "I talked to our local federal government export folks and they told us about the Export-Import Bank of the U.S. We applied and were accepted into the Bank's loan guarantee program, which provides working capital to U.S. exporters at competitive rates. With the Bank's assistance and that of the U.S. Commercial Service you can't stop us. We can go anywhere. Since 2005, when we made our first export, the company has set up distribution on five continents and sold products to customers in 41 countries—so far. And we're about to add a couple of new ones today."

The founder of a small minority-owned engineering company specializing in setting up laboratories for the study of diseases called on the government to help her export for the first time. "As a small business you're going to need somebody who knows how to do business in that country. For the connections, you have to know people. It's great advice that I received from the Department of Commerce and the Small Business Administration that is really making a difference in our pursuit of opportunities abroad."

"The mentality of Americans is to be satisfied with the North American market. That's just plain shortsighted."

Another service provider made this observation: "We have advanced work in Brazil, Argentina, and Colombia that came as a major benefit of working with the U.S. Commerce Department, which offers an exposition called Trade Winds. It connects us with personnel at U.S. embassies. These events and meetings give us the ability to evaluate markets on a case-by-case basis and then pick the best targets of opportunity. We've gone in there to identify service partners, professional services, import-export laws."

Another manufacturer said that rather than a one-shot deal, he's been using government services to grow his company for more than three decades: "Thirty years ago I called [the U.S. government]. Don't remember why. It was telexes then, and the international trade specialist sent a bunch to her colleagues at the embassies. I got inundated with requests from potential buyers, and I got into all kinds of markets. Thirty years later I'm still using them."

One of the exporters praised a different kind of government assistance. He said that unemployment insurance helped him retrain to create a new business during a deep recession, and tax credits for hiring new workers for his new export business helped the business become profitable faster.

Government help is not the only kind of assistance these exporters use. Some of them have used consultants to good effect, especially in finding franchising partners. Others have hired international marketing specialists as part of their leadership team. And a number of companies have done all three.

These, then, are the seven themes that emerge from one possible reading of the stories: exporting as a key to growth; rich learning; exporting companies are good at business fundamentals; a belief that the world is flat; the advantages of manufacturing in the U.S.; the immigrant myth that isn't; and a willingness to engage U.S. government export assistance programs. You are welcome to draw your own conclusions and, most importantly, to see if exporting or expanding exports are things you want to do. As one of the exporters said, "I'm 67 now and have been doing this for a long time. I still love it. I see so much opportunity out there. All we as Americans have to do is go there and do it."

Turn the page, and here we go!

The Stories

Ron Swinko
Chief Executive Officer, Jet Incorporated

How did the company get started and what does it do?

The company was founded in 1955. The basic equipment that the company designed at that time was to replace septic tanks with advanced technology, to treat the water using a smaller system, and to allow the water to be discharged. That was the foundation of the company. And over the years we expanded into commercial systems which are typically called small-package plants for decentralized locations—small villages, hotels, resorts, those types of things. That is the basis for our international growth as well.

For the nonscientists, can you give us a quick overview of how things work?

It's biological wastewater treatment. So anything that comes from either the sinks or the sanitary systems in a home or in a building, the water enters into the system, into a tank, where the solids are digested by aerobic bacteria. And part of our system is designed to inject air that promotes the growth of that aerobic bacteria. The resulting water that's discharged is clean and odorless and, depending upon the application, can be simply dispersed underground, or it can be disinfected in one additional step and reused for irrigation, for crops, for nonhuman consumption, or for watering flower gardens, golf courses. In some cases, we've had our systems produce water that's reused in a steel manufacturing process.

What are aerobic bacteria? Sounds like Zumba for microbes.

They are bacteria that grow as a result of oxygen being present in the water.

How did the international part of the business begin, and what was the biggest challenge in getting going?

It started with inquiries because of the technology that was developed. The founder, David MacLaren, was certainly an innovator. And he was also very interested in expanding the technology internationally. He obtained a series of patents in several countries over the years.

Distributor training in Kenya

What we found was that the most significant challenge was servicing our international distributors. And by servicing, that certainly means having enough inventory to meet their demands for immediate shipment, understanding what the export requirements are, and ultimately providing solid technical support for systems that have been installed. We look at international development as one of our challenges to educate internationally.

Developing countries may be focused on environmental sustainability even to a greater extent than we are here in the U.S. because of the scarcity of water. But they may not necessarily understand the benefit of regulation or the type of equipment that's available. And as a result, over the last couple of years, one of our initiatives has been to educate regulators in, for example, the Cayman Islands and in Kenya. We hosted a seminar on wastewater management for the architects' association of Kenya to at least provide some education into how wastewater treatment systems can generate water for reuse and how that can be incorporated into sustainable projects for buildings, for example—apartment buildings, resorts.

In response to that challenge, which was getting your products and services known in the international markets, finding distributors and informing them and the regulators, who did you turn to in order to find a solution?

We've used the U.S. Commercial Service quite extensively. They have a wonderful service called the Gold Key, and because our business relies on increasing the number of distributors, we look for partners in developing countries who will act as distributors and who are technically capable, either because they're currently in the water purification business or because they're in the construction business. We have been very successful in using Gold Key and also the advice of the U.S. Commercial Service to expand, particularly into Southeast Asia and into South America. I just recently returned from a trade mission to Brazil that included four Gold Key meetings with potential distributors in São Paolo.

When you say Gold Key, do you provide the gold and they provide the key?

It's more mutual than that. But truthfully, the U.S. Commercial Service spends a great deal of time learning about our business, learning about our company and the requirements for distributors in the location, and then evaluates potential distributor partners and partner companies in that area. They establish the meetings after they've reviewed the capabilities and what our requirements are and look for a match, a good match I would say, maybe in terms of company personality as well as technical expertise.

Let's talk about the matches in Brazil. It would have been hard for you to fly in unannounced to Rio and São Paolo and open a phone book. So they had a solution for that. But how did it work out on the ground? Are you confident that good things will come of those meetings?

Very confident. Part of the service includes an interpreter. So if there are any language barriers, particularly with technical terms or equipment, the interpreters are very capable. But for the most part, they also look for companies that have good language skills in terms of English and an understanding of English. We're quite confident that this was an excellent trip for us. We've already had more detailed discussions with two of the companies and we've already had three quotes for systems requested. The trade mission itself was particularly impressive in terms of the level of government officials that we met with, and the management level of the potential customers or clients that we met with, as well—so very, very important and detailed technical presentations on their environmental sustainability programs—and certainly from our perspective well worth the participation and the trip.

Give us a snapshot of how many employees you have at present and what percentage of the business is international and how it's grown and is growing.

We have about 30 employees. All of our manufacturing is done in our Cleveland, Ohio, location. The business in the U.S. is highly dependent on residential construction. So during the last several years, of course, the housing industry has struggled—which would be putting it mildly. It's been significantly challenged, and while we have done reasonably well domestically, internationally the expansion has allowed us to actually increase the number of employees and add an additional engineer so that we could continue to support the international business.

International is about 25 percent of our business, with some nice year-over-year growth in the 30-plus-percent range.

Where do you see it going in the future?

I would say certainly maintaining those particular increases, especially because of demand from the markets where we have a significant presence, like Africa, as well as the South American countries.

Are China and India on the horizon?

China, no—partly because of some intellectual property concerns but also because we have such a strong presence in these other developing countries where we haven't fully leveraged the market.

Why are you not among the U.S. companies that outsource your manufacturing?

The foundation of the company is Cleveland, and that has been the location since 1955. So there is a strong commitment to manufacturing as much as we can in the U.S. Quite honestly, there are some very distinct challenges with that because certain manufacturing processes and products are not available in the U.S., or if they are, they're available at a high price multiple compared to what you can purchase overseas. But we do also try to work within NAFTA as well so we keep the supply chain as short as we can.

Is there a value in "Made in America" with your international customers?

Without a doubt there is, especially in the environmental technologies equipment market. Our distributors and customers overseas greatly respect the regulation that we've had over the years that's improved our air and water. And "Made in America," or designed in America or serviced by Americans, in many of these countries has a very strong, positive connotation.

Can it make up for the premium pricing that is required?

In many cases it can. Buyers are very sensitive to where things are made, and they will evaluate a purchase on the basis of whether, and how many of your components may have been, made outside of the U.S.

If you were asked to advise all these millions of U.S. companies that are making useful things or have useful services to deliver that aren't looking outside the U.S. for additional business, what would you tell them?

I would tell them that there is a terrific resource in the Department of Commerce, and the U.S. Commercial Service is probably one of the most underappreciated—except by the companies that utilize the service. There are terrific benefits, great skill sets both in the U.S. and internationally with their staff on the ground in the other countries who do a great job of evaluating the markets and prospective clients. And it's very economical.

And when they say, "We're from the U.S. government and we're here to help you," you don't fall on the floor laughing?

No, we don't. We say, "Thank you, we've used you before and you are welcome to help us again."

Would you say that you are a better company as the result of your international experience?

I would say we're certainly a better company, and we're a better company because each of those countries, while they can use the basic equipment, do require some modification, do require particular levels of service. And so it's really driven some of our innovation of the equipment systems that have produced superior systems for all of our markets, domestic and international. It's without a doubt caused us to rethink how we train our distributors. We used to train our distributors after they received their first order, and about a year or so ago we decided that they were challenged because they didn't fully understand the technology in order to go sell the equipment. So we reversed the normal process and now we train them, very completely, with an on-site visit before their first sale. And that also allows them to use the technical staff to go out and perhaps close a sale. So we've really refocused on education, not only of our distributors but also of the local regulators within the countries. What we're doing is we're educating them about what's achievable. But their focus on the water usage and reuse is really driven by the scarcity of water. So while they may not have the regulation, they are very strongly committed to water conservation. And, as a result, they're extremely interested in technologies that can treat water effectively and provide water for reuse.

Can you give a concrete example of an innovation that has occurred as a result of something you learned in interacting with a foreign customer?

One of the things that we've learned is that we have to be very, very careful on the detail of information that we request before we do the quotation and before we design the system.

If the questions are not detailed enough, people will quite often forget what may be a significant contributor to the influent, the water that enters into the system. And that can create some significant challenges for treating the water, whether it's in terms of volume or in terms of the amount of waste that's in the water itself.

Is this country specific, culture specific?

It is more culture specific. Clients may not have particular regulations. They may forget about a particular contribution to the influent. And so, you know, we've refined our questionnaires. We've added some capabilities for proving—proof of concept of the design of the system before we even manufacture and install the equipment.

And these innovations have allowed you to ask these questions of other places where you go to do business in other countries?

Yes.

Do these innovations also apply to your U.S. domestic sales? Has it improved the systems that you make here?

They do. In many cases, internationally, the available energy is not as regular. There are power interruptions. In some countries, the preference is for solar power or low-energy-use pieces of equipment. So that is currently driving some of our development programs. ⊘

Elena Stegemann
International Sales Manager, NuStep

When did the company start and what do you make?

The company started about 20 years ago. Our owner and CEO, Dick Sams, is a biomedical engineer. He had another company before this one. He is one of the creators of one of the first heart-lung machines in the world. So he had a company under a different name which he took global. After he sold that business and after he had been immersed in the experience of working with people who had cardiac problems and needed a heart-lung machine, he decided to focus with his next company on the prevention of heart disease. So one aspect of prevention, we now know, is exercise. But 30 years ago, that was not a well-known fact. So Dick Sams is really a pioneer in this area and sometimes is referred to as the grandfather of biomedical engineering. He had an idea: to help change people's lives through exercise and movement.

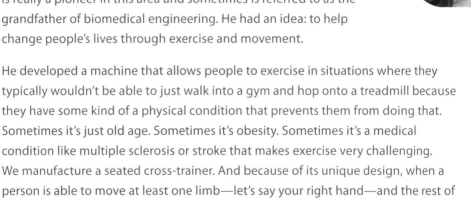

He developed a machine that allows people to exercise in situations where they typically wouldn't be able to just walk into a gym and hop onto a treadmill because they have some kind of a physical condition that prevents them from doing that. Sometimes it's just old age. Sometimes it's obesity. Sometimes it's a medical condition like multiple sclerosis or stroke that makes exercise very challenging. We manufacture a seated cross-trainer. And because of its unique design, when a person is able to move at least one limb—let's say your right hand—and the rest of your body is paralyzed, because of the design of the machine, once you move your right hand, everything else moves in a passive response.

This is very unique because some of the people who use our equipment can't use their legs. Some people have not seen their legs move either ever or in a very long time. And they are able to sit down, get on a NuStep. Their legs get strapped in with special adaptive devices that allow them to be comfortably locked in an ergonomically correct position. Then they start using their hands and, lo and behold, their legs are moving. As NuStep's international business manager, I get to travel around the world and introduce people to this product, and it's been a great privilege of mine to see people who have clearly not seen their legs move in a very long time, to see that happen for the first time. You have to understand it's not just a physical transformation. It's everything about that person changes in that one moment. So we get to bring those moments to people now around the world, not just in the U.S.

So the creation of this company didn't happen overnight, nor did you instantly find markets for the product outside of the U.S. What was the company's biggest challenge in bringing this technology to a global market?

It definitely didn't happen overnight. It's been the result of the sustained efforts of our entire team over the course of several years. I would say the biggest challenge that we face on a daily basis entering new markets is the mind-set that people have in other parts of the world that exercise is not necessarily how we think of it. We now kind of almost intuitively accept the idea that exercise is a critical aspect of the well-being of every person—young, old, healthy, disabled, whoever you are. You need to have exercise in your life.

> "When you're present and mindful, you see . . . precursors to trends that will eventually come to the U.S."

There are many people around the world who really have not embraced this idea yet. So when I travel to, let's say, the United Kingdom (UK), this is a real example. We think of the UK, again intuitively as well, that it's a natural market for us to go into. We speak the same language. We have a similar cultural heritage. "Sure, let's take our product there. They'll get it immediately." Not so. You walk into a senior living or assisted-care facility in the UK and typically you see that it's not designed for exercise. They'll have a beauty parlor. They'll have a games room. They'll have beautiful grounds, but there is nowhere in the design and the layout of the facility that shows that the architect or the owner, whoever created this building, set aside space for exercise. They're just not thinking about that as an important aspect for the residents who are living there. So when I walk in there and I try to tell them about this, you know, "exciting opportunity for their residents," they look at me like I'm crazy. "What? You want grandma to exercise, she has worked hard her whole life, she needs to sit on the couch and drink tea and watch the telly, right?"

And the same thing is true with people who are in hospitals and have had some kind of medical trauma in their lives. Again, the natural instinct of the people who care for them is that they should rest, they should not be exerting themselves. They shouldn't be sweating and moving and, you know, they need to lie down. We need to protect them. This is our number one challenge.

The response to this challenge is to provide up-front education of prospective customers directly or via your in-country suppliers—creating awareness of how exercise is going to help people instead of damaging them.

Training is important, but not easy to do when you are a small company in the middle of the U.S. and your prospective customers, whoever they may be, are thousands of miles away. Early on, when I took on the role of international business manager for the company, one of the things I was tasked with is creation of a go-to-market strategy. How are we going to do this? How is this little company in Ann Arbor, Michigan, going to reach out to the rest of the world? And we had to recognize, that being a small company, we didn't have offices around the world. We didn't have a global team of salespeople who were going to knock on doors and do this on our behalf. Early on, I made the decision that we were going to work with distributors around the world and were going to build up a team of really sophisticated visionary-type distributor companies who really got the idea and understood the challenge that they were going to have in creating awareness for our product in their market, yet saw the huge opportunity for them.

They were going to be willing to put in the time, the effort, the resources necessary to educate their market and create awareness for our product. So our number one challenge was, and continues to be as we expand our presence, to find those partners globally. This is where the U.S. Commercial Service has been an invaluable resource to us. The folks at the U.S. Commercial Service office in Pontiac, Michigan—Richard Corson and Jennifer Loffredo—have become very good friends of mine. They have been doing this with me since I started in January of 2009. They introduced their services to me. There's a whole slew of services available, depending on how comfortable you are doing these things on your own, what kind of help you need.

You, the U.S. company, kind of pick and choose. It's a whole menu. It's like going out to a restaurant. So Jennifer and Richard have basically opened the door for me to the global network of Commercial Service specialists around the world to talk about whatever issue is keeping me up at night worrying what are we going to do in China or Brazil, and wherever. They have facilitated conference calls for me in São Paolo, Brazil, dealing with an issue with a particular distributor where they actually advised me against working with someone who, if I had worked with, I think we would have ended up being in a lot of trouble. They facilitated a conference call and follow-up emails and all kinds of help with a distributor in Korea. So I talked to the Seoul team on intellectual property (IP) issues and other things with finding a distributor, checking somebody out to make sure they were capable and honest. That's actually been a big one where I think I have the company that I want to work with. I'm not sure exactly. I don't have the cultural sensitivity to understand whether some of the odd signals that I'm getting from them are just cultural and are perfectly normal or if there is something fishy going on there.

I've tapped into the capability of the folks at the U.S. Commercial Service to have the local team check out the distributor, vet them for me, and say: "Yeah, these guys, you know, whatever weirdness you're getting from them, that's actually how people interact in that part of the world. They're OK." Or actually, like the people in Brazil, I was able to get some information that the U.S. Commercial Service got from the embassy that really ended up helping me make the decision to not work with people who would have gotten me into trouble. So access to those people on the ground there is like having your own consultant network for free or very low cost. How great is that?

And then the other part that has played a big role for us and our success is MEDICA—a huge medical equipment trade show in Germany. We went there in 2009. We wanted to be in Germany. We wanted to be in other European countries. This was the place where I met a lot of people. We were treated like royalty by the U.S. government staff who worked at the USA Pavilion. We had our own interpreter. He made appointments for us. They brought us coffee. I felt like a CEO, which is the name of the program. We ended up having conversations with distributors from different countries. And as a result of those meetings, we ended up having agreements—distributorship agreements that are still in place in Germany, Australia, and Italy. Not bad, OK? So this was the first year that we decided to go international. And if we hadn't gone to MEDICA and hadn't used the U.S. Commercial Service, I think that would have delayed us by several years.

What kind of business did you generate through all those activities?

We ended up getting three agreements in place. They didn't all happen right there and then. It allowed us to meet with people, have real conversations, not just once, but because we were there we had a presence there for the three or four days that the show is there. We were able to have the initial conversation with lots of people and then kind of screen out those that we didn't like, make follow-up appointments with people that looked kind of serious and were potentially a good fit. And when we left, we kind of felt like, "OK, you know, these are the companies that we feel very serious about. Let's have a real conversation with them now about pricing, logistics, and how they will promote our product."

Because our product is unique—it's expensive—it's not immediately obvious to people how they're going to sell it. There is generally a delay between the time that we make the agreement to work together and the time that the product actually arrives there in containers and they're actually selling it to customers. So there was a delay of probably 6 months to 18 months in getting agreements signed, depending on the country. But the important thing is we locked in three distributors who get our product. They're good enough for us to work with.

Your product could be classified as either exercise equipment or medical equipment, which involves more foreign government regulation. Does this pose a challenge?

This is an ongoing challenge for us because in some markets our product is actually considered to be a medical device. So we have to meet European Community (CE) requirements or whatever the local requirements may be for a medical device. And then, in other countries, we're not a medical device.

In other countries we're just exercise equipment and that's not regulated. So one of our challenges is knowing before we enter a market: What's it going to be; do we meet their requirements? If we don't, how difficult will it be; how much will it cost? This is also an area where the U.S. Commercial Service has been of great help to us because their people are in more than 70 countries. Not to pick on Brazil too much, but they are a bit of a challenge in terms of . . . exporting. Not surprisingly, they have their own version of the CE mark for medical products. They have something called Anvisa—and again, not surprisingly, it's not easy. It's not a slam-dunk to get that certification. So the U.S. Commercial Service was able to give us some guidelines there for Brazil. And we had to take a step back and say, "Whoa, you know, we're not sure we're ready to make the financial commitment to have our product go through this testing because we don't have a distributor yet and we're not sure and perhaps we need to find the distributor first." So knowing what type of a regulatory system our product falls under has been definitely a major consideration in our expansion efforts.

> *". . . being a businesswoman and dipping [my] toe in the waters . . . is a transformational opportunity not only for myself, but also for other people that I interact with.*

What do international sales mean to your company?

We are now in 25 countries, which is pretty good. Our international business is now about 15 percent of our revenue. So if we didn't have that, it would hurt. It's a significant portion of our business and growing. This is over a period of three-and-a-half to four years. We've just started. And that's 15 percent, from almost nothing. You can imagine, with that kind of momentum, that's becoming a greater and bigger portion of our business every year. So we've added people. We're hiring people. We're keeping other people employed, not just in our company, but other people working with trucking, logistics, banking, letters of credit, packaging; all kinds of people are working because we are shipping containers of stuff.

It's interesting that your company hires displaced auto workers.

We have a great location in Ann Arbor, Michigan. If you've ever been there, it's beautiful. It's a college town, a little bubble of economic prosperity. But the reality is we're right next door to Detroit. And, of course, everybody knows about the challenges that we've had in Detroit keeping people working. If Detroit is suffering, we feel it too. So because of what happened with the automotive industry and actually even other employers, even in Ann Arbor, we lost Pfizer, which was a big employer. It's a big pharmaceutical company. Borders, the bookseller, they were headquartered in Ann Arbor too, and they shut their doors.

Because we are growing, we are able to re-employ some of these people. Because we're a manufacturer, we actually bend steel. We cut. We weld. We do the good old-fashioned American manufacturing thing; we need people who can do that. And, fortunately for us, right next door to us is the great city of Detroit where all these people were formerly bending and cutting and welding to make cars. Lucky for us, we can tap into their experience and of keep that great American tradition of manufacturing going; but now we're manufacturing healthcare equipment. We're benefiting from their expertise. And, through our efforts, we're helping people in other parts of the world to live a better life. Yeah, pretty exciting!

> *"How is this little company in Ann Arbor, Michigan, going to reach out to the rest of the world?*

As you've traveled around to nursing homes and hospitals throughout the world, have you learned things that have made your company a better company?

Absolutely. It's been kind of an unexpected benefit for us because when I go to trade shows, when I go to visit with customers or potential customers in other countries, they're asking me questions, like, "Well, can your product do this, can you do that?" And sometimes the answer is "yes." Sometimes it's like, "I don't know; we've never thought of that because in the U.S. no one has ever asked us this question."

I feel like being a global company is giving us a competitive advantage over other companies who are not necessarily present internationally. When you're present and mindful, you see things going on there that are precursors to trends that will eventually come to the U.S. So we sometimes have the opportunity to see the future. It's like a crystal ball, and you have to be observant. I take a lot of pictures with my smartphone, and people in my company rely on me to quickly text or send a picture. "Hey, I'm at this hospital; look at what I'm seeing, isn't that interesting?" And I'll shoot that over and people will take a look and say, "Huh, well that is interesting." So it's definitely allowing us to be a better company and have a competitive edge.

Can you give us an example of one innovation or change that you made on your device as a result of something you observed somewhere?

We are working on something that I am not at liberty to share. But it came about in part because I kept on going to international trade shows and I was seeing, observing a trend that is much more prevalent in Europe that is something that's not very interesting to people in our market right now. But our product development group has embraced it as something that will be incorporated into the next version of our product. And I apologize that I am not at liberty to disclose it.

During your trip here you went to the White House to receive a Presidential E-Award for excellence in exporting, and you were telling me earlier that you were born in the former Soviet Union. You went first to Canada and then to the U.S. It must be amazing to see yourself going from pariah to being honored at the White House.

It's been an amazing journey. It makes you think that there's some invisible hand guiding you throughout life. When I was a child living in the former Soviet Union, at the time we were definitely enemies with the U.S. I was living in an environment where we weren't allowed to access information about the U.S. and the rest of the world. I remember my dad listening to the Voice of America in the middle of the night because if he was doing it during the day, the neighbors might hear and he would get into serious trouble. My dad told me very clearly that I wasn't allowed to tell anybody that he listened to the Voice of America. Growing up as a child in that environment, the U.S. was like another planet. If somebody had told me back then that I was going to be a U.S. citizen one day, that I was going to travel and represent the U.S. one day with an American passport and that I would end up in the White House one day, I would have just laughed. I mean, it was just so incredibly unbelievable!

So sitting there at the White House, it was definitely a very emotional moment for me. And I was thinking about how proud I am to represent American companies. And I do feel a little bit like an ambassador when I travel to different parts of the world. Sometimes Americans have this bad reputation. But people do love Americans. I've got to tell you how many times I have been introduced as the lady from America—many, many times in many languages. And it's because it opens doors. People do love Americans. Whatever the governments are doing, whatever disagreements happen at that level, people are fascinated by Americans, just the way I was as a kid. And so now I get to be the person from America. And people open their doors for me because of that. Life is amazing! And wow, I just feel very lucky! Sorry, I'm a little bit emotional and maybe not very coherent.

What about being a woman ambassador of business? Is it an advantage, a disadvantage, or does it matter at all?

It can be all of those. It's just like anything else in life. It depends on your perspective on things. I see that as an advantage. So I just treat it as such. Whether it is or it isn't is up to the other person to decide. I think that in some countries, let's say Scandinavia where we have a distribution network, I would call them very progressive from that standpoint. It wouldn't occur to them to think that I'm not an equal in any sense because I'm a woman. It's just not part of the mind-set. I was a little bit nervous, I remember, going to Japan for the first time because I had done some homework. I had read up on their culture—how women are still kind of kept out of the corporate world. But when I walked in and I was there to do business, I was excited and happy to be there. I had prepared, I had done my homework, and I had shown them respect by taking their culture very seriously—the respect was reciprocated.

So whatever was going on inside of their heads, whatever discomfort they may have felt at being with a woman—and in fact, the first time I went, I traveled with my boss, a male, who's a VP in our company and they kept on talking to him and asking him questions. And he would then ask me for the answer. And I could see the confusion in their faces the first day or so. They just didn't know how to deal with that. But eventually they got over it. So that was a great experience. But my absolute favorite time was when I went to Dubai last year. And it was my first time in the Middle East, and so I knew that Dubai was progressive in terms of women participating in business. But still, a little bit apprehensive. And I had the opportunity to meet with a group of maybe four or five businessmen from Saudi Arabia.

I knew that the culture in Saudi Arabia is very different in terms of women participating in business. So I was very apprehensive about that. I dressed very modestly. I tried to be anticipatory in the way things were going to go. And I was completely surprised—very positively— by the interactions that I ended up having with these gentlemen. We had a business meeting. It was very natural, very comfortable. And the entire time I kept expecting that it's going to become like what I thought it was going to be. That they're going to say, "OK great, but let me talk to your boss, the man." There was none of that. Then we went out to lunch and we had a lovely time together.

> *"...being a global company is giving us a competitive advantage over other companies who are not necessarily present internationally."*

They were very proud of their culture. They explained, you know, this dessert. It's called "oum Ali," which means the mother of Ali. And it was like being with the Scandinavian businesspeople. And when I walked away from there, I thought to myself, "Oh my God, this lunch totally shattered whatever preconceived notions I had about Saudi men." And I'm thinking it probably did something to their idea about American women, too. And maybe about women in general, that here we had a really good conversation. I didn't do anything crazy or whatever they worry about women doing and why they don't allow women to do business, I don't know. But I think it was kind of a transformational moment for all of us during that time. And I keep on thinking about it, like wow! So being a businesswoman and dipping your toe in the waters and stepping out is a transformational opportunity not only for myself, but also for other people that I interact with.

It was all fine until you said to the Saudi men: "Let me drive you back to the office?"
Yes. And they said, "Where is your brother?" ⬦

Mark Rice
Owner, Maritime Applied Physics

How did you get started?

We're a 25-year-old company. We have about 10 research and development contracts and 5 production contracts at the same time. We have been exporting for about 10 years now. We build marine components for ships as well as some advanced marine vehicles. So we build unmanned boats for the U.S. Navy. Some of our exports have been large rudder systems and bridge controls in South Korea. We've designed an America's Cup hull for the Italians. We've done some advanced battery work in France. And we currently have a project in Scotland, where we're building a control system for a large piece of marine machinery.

Less than 2 percent of all U.S. companies export. What made you part of that less than 2 percent?

We were originally an accidental exporter. We were contacted by a business agent from South Korea who found that we had done a project for the U.S. Navy that was very similar to one that was starting in South Korea. He called and asked us to come to South Korea to Hyundai Heavy Industries, the largest shipyard in the world. So we decided to get on a plane and go, and ended up in a bidding war against a UK company that lasted about 9 months. At the end of that process, we won the bid against a much larger company and struck out on the adventure of exporting.

What was the bid worth?

The bid was $2,300,000, which was about equal to 50 percent of our revenue at that point, so it was a huge export in terms of percentage.

You referred to yourself as an accidental exporter. That's probably how a lot of companies would classify themselves. And you had internal discussions about whether to export or not. What was the mind-set at the time? And what was involved in those internal discussions?

I think when we were first contacted we were intrigued, but probably had zero knowledge to base our decision on. So as we went through the process, we stumbled through a bunch of things and made a lot of mistakes. We almost violated the International Trafficking in Arms Regulations and got between the Departments of Commerce and State on that. That was our first problem.

As we went into the bidding, I guess we got drawn into it. The competition took on a "We've-got-to-beat-you-guys" sort of attitude. And so we made actually three trips to South Korea during that process. And in each case the person who had originally contacted us gave us a little bit more of the South Korean culture and we adapted, I think, over the process of the three trips.

What were the most challenging cultural things that you ran into, and how did you overcome them?

I think we were largely people who had not traveled internationally, so this was a whole new culture for us and a new experience. In South Korea, businesses perform very differently than in the U.S. The cultural norms of how to do business, what's expected of you, what isn't, was a constant issue. Much to the chagrin of our business partner there, we made many mistakes as we went through this process, but found, as in most business relationships, a smile and a "thank you" and an "I'm sorry" every once in a while made up for all these things.

At the end of the day, it was our technical background that really won the project. We went through a bidding process that was on 3-by-5 cards across a table that lasted for several days, where our price was always too high. By the time we were finished, we were told that we were half a million dollars below our UK competitor. So it was an intense process; the etiquette of that bidding process was really different. We had been used to U.S. processes and it was radically different.

Was there a memorable cultural faux pas/mistake that you made that can be generalized to other U.S. companies?

Probably the biggest mistake was in the bidding process. We were expected to start high and work our way down a significant amount. And, you know, we were told in the first round of the bid: "Give us your best price." And we did that, which gave us very little room to lower our price. And that, according to our business partner, was an insult to the client company. So that was probably the most difficult part of the negotiation.

Why did they ask for your best price when they didn't expect it? Did they think their ship might come in?

That's the culture. There's a theatrical, ritualistic aspect to it and you need to know that going in.

How do you know that?

Ask. You need not be alone in these interactions. Call our embassy. Call the Department of Commerce International Trade Administration.

What happened after you won the bid?

I would say, the other part, as we won the contract and engaged in it, we learned shipyards are strange social organizations to begin with. There are tens of thousands of workers eating in cafeterias. We were pushed right into the food line in a South Korean cafeteria that was serving 3,000 employees. We were all in uniforms and we stuck out like a sore thumb as we were served our *kimchi* [fermented cabbage] and rice for lunch. But you quickly found that it was a wonderful experience. I mean, our people grew immensely from the whole experience. We didn't make a lot of money, but we got through the warranty period with no major failures, and that launched us into the exciting part of exporting. I think, at this point, we're anxious to seek out those opportunities around the world. Each one's a new adventure and opportunity to meet new people and understand new cultures.

> "Don't fear that world. You have a partner in the Department of Commerce that will help you go overseas."

It's intriguing that you mention the personal growth side of things and what you learn through direct experience. How have these experiences working in different cultures benefited the people in your company just by going outside their comfort zone?

I think one of the things that we noticed right away in South Korea is all our counterpart engineers on the other side of the table were experienced in exporting. They dealt with shipowners from all over the world. We came in and this was our first experience. So we were at a real disadvantage, engineer to engineer, in these relationships. And I think that comfort level with dealing on an international basis with another engineer, exchanging information, what are the cultural norms and how do you build friendships and business relationships, was really what changed our people. So our people came away from that experience perhaps not as culturally savvy as our South Korean counterparts were, but at least not as insular as they were when they left the U.S.

Is it confidence, a certain kind of skill set, or both?

I think it's the fear barrier, right? It's confidence and the ability to take on something that you're not sure of—probably similar to what you learn in terms of engineering skills and attacking a new problem. Engineers that I've dealt with over my career are rather insular and have relatively few business capabilities coming out of school. Pushing them into an international business relationship is a quick way to go from zero to 100 miles an hour. Every aspect of the trip and the relationship and the expectations and the cultural norms are different. They challenge the engineers to get out of their established ways.

You urge other businesses to seek help from U.S. government agencies and say that you would have benefited if you had done so prior to the negotiation experience. What agencies have you used? Not everyone these days is rushing into the arms of government organizations.

Prior to our first interaction with the U.S. Commercial Service we had dealt mainly with the Department of Defense and other government agencies, where we were the contractor serving a government agency. And what was remarkably different about the U.S. Commercial Service is all of a sudden that was turned 180 degrees around. They were the people there to serve. And the extent to which they would work to help us was remarkable and very different than anything we'd ever had in an industry-government relationship. So it was very clear from the first day that if we have a problem, we pick the phone up, we talk to our local U.S. Commercial Service office.

In the case of the South Korean contract, we came back from South Korea and our bank said, "This is too risky a deal. We're going to withdraw our credit lines from your company." So we had to go find a new bank. And key to that was the U.S. Commercial Service introducing us to the U.S. Small Business Administration and ultimately getting a 90 percent loan guarantee on the project. And that enabled us not only to do the job, but to survive that whole crisis. So in terms of relationships with government agencies, I've never seen an industry-government relationship that's as helpful to a company as the one that the U.S. Commercial Service offers. It's remarkable.

It sounds like the banks need to go through a transformative experience much as you did at the Korean shipyard.

Absolutely. The banks are, you know, insular in their own right. And they do not generally understand international business. And in general they're reluctant to loan to companies that are doing international business. Some of the larger, more centralized banks have good international departments, but by the time you get out of those central areas it's pretty hard to find a banker who understands letters of credit and all the peculiarities of delivering goods.

What advice do you have for the many thousands of companies that might have something to offer the rest of the world?

Certainly, don't fear that world. You have a partner in the Department of Commerce that will help you go overseas. Many states provide assistance to exporters. And the market is huge. If you have a product that's solid and you are selling that in the U.S., there's a good chance that you can compete—at least in some parts of the world. And if you're really thinking of the U.S. as your market, you're missing a huge opportunity in terms of sales. And it may actually be a very necessary step that you take for your own survival as well as your growth. So have no fear. Go forward and engage and use the U.S. government to help you in these things. And enjoy the great cultural experiences that will come with that. ⌀

Michelle Khalatian
Vice President, International Marketing, Falcon Waterfree Technologies

How did the company get started?

A water shortage spurred the idea. Perhaps 5 percent of fresh water is literally flushed away in urinals around the world. There had to be a better way, or so thought Ditmar Gorges, coinventor of a water-free urinal. Thanks to him and his company, Falcon Waterfree Technologies, the little cartridges that absorb urine without the need for water are becoming a staple in male restrooms across the globe.

It took more than a good idea to build a successful business and a patented product. Gorges, a mechanical engineer by training, went back to school for a master's degree in economics. The company began, with the intent of retrofitting toilets and saving users a lot of money in water and sewer fees. Water is scarce and becoming scarcer in many parts of the world, and it's too costly in economic and environmental terms to flush it down the drain. [Gorges] was sitting in a Los Angeles bar having a beer, talking to some engineer friends, during a water shortage and mandatory water rationing. He put 2 and 2 together.

From these small beginnings, Falcon Waterfree now has offices in Grand Rapids, Michigan, and Los Angeles, California, where the research and development are done, and the products sell in 55 countries worldwide with a staff of about 60 in the U.S. and worldwide. Our product can be found in some surprising places, including India's Taj Mahal, where a solution was needed that didn't require installing piping in ancient walls, and the Austrian Alps, where we had the distinction of outfitting the highest restroom in the world.

On average, each Falcon Waterfree urinal saves up to 40,000 gallons or more of fresh water per year. With over 350,000 Falcon urinals installed throughout the world, Falcon Waterfree Technologies directly saves approximately 14 billion gallons of water each year.

How did international sales get started?

Falcon Waterfree began selling in foreign countries in 1995. The company had two competitors in the U.S., six in Europe, and at that time none in Asia, where we are hurrying to take advantage of an open playing field: a 100 percent market share of retrofitted waterless urinals and infinite growth in public restrooms. Falcon Waterfree's number-one position seems secure for the moment because our technology is different from the competition's, and customers tell us that ours is easier to use. Falcon Waterfree's sales worldwide are increasing about 140 percent per year. Our technology seems bulletproof at the moment, but we need to constantly improve.

"Falcon Waterfree's sales worldwide are increasing about 140 percent per year."

In 2012 we launched a new cartridge, the C1M2+, which represents our continual focus on product improvement. Falcon prides itself on improving its technology to make sure that it is offering the most technologically advanced water-free system in the market. We have made internal changes to the architecture of the cartridge which result in using less sealant, but being more resistant to bucket dumps or washouts. On the top, we eliminate the diverter shield due to the internal changes. The purpose of the teardrop or football-shaped device on top of the cartridge is that it aids in the flow of fluid into the cartridge. Our experience revealed that the diverter cap was often the source of odor due to inadequate maintenance. Through internal design improvements to the cartridge, we no longer require the diverter cap and, have improved the resistance of the cartridge to bucket dumps. As always, all Falcon innovations are backward compatible, meaning they can be used in earlier urinal models. Falcon has put over 3 years of work into reengineering our cartridge. This has resulted in extensive product development costs, including new molds. Falcon would be justified in taking a price increase for this improved product, but instead is holding prices at the current level. We are also very proud of the fact that this new cartridge is now "Made in America." This, of course, allows countries with free-trade agreements with the U.S. to enjoy the benefits of not paying duties and taxes for the product, previously made in China. During the last few years we've succeeded in making the cartridges long lasting and 100 percent recyclable.

Ditmar Gorges (center) in Beijing with members of the U.S. Commercial Service.

What about the urinals themselves?

Most are manufactured in the market. Manufacturing locally allows distributors and end customers to enjoy competitive pricing. Shipping heavy porcelain all over the world simply does not make sense when we can have manufacturing locations in strategic regions, including Latin America, Europe, and Asia. Typical is an agreement we just signed with a company in Colombia. Corona S.A. is a multinational Colombian company with over 130 years of experience. It is comprised of six strategic business units, dedicated to manufacturing and distribution of home and building products. Corona has 17 manufacturing locations in Colombia and 2 in the U.S., along with a global supply center based in China and a distributor operation in Mexico. They export their products around the world, in such markets as USA, Canada, Mexico, Brazil, Chile, Venezuela, Central America, the Caribbean, Italy, Spain, and the United Kingdom. Through this and other efforts we'll further establish the Falcon brand in Colombia, Ecuador, Belize, El Salvador, Guatemala, Honduras, Nicaragua, Panama, Puerto Rico, and the Dominican Republic.

> "Our technology seems bulletproof at the moment, but we need to constantly improve."

Corona will manufacture the urinals, add the cartridge, and provide training to the buyers.

Yes. This is one model, as is just selling the cartridges. We currently sell through distributors in most countries. There might be an exception here and there. Our goal is to work with partners that are market leaders in their territory. We are open to new ideas in terms of urinal models as we have learned over the years that shape and size is region specific due to cultural preferences. I will say that one region that has been challenging for Falcon is Brazil. We have yet to find a partner in the region, but would very much like to get into that market. We are in China. We hired a VP of sales, Paul Liang, who is based in Taiwan, to focus on this region. We are opening a new office and see this as a very important region for Falcon's expansion.

How have you worked with U.S. government export assistance services?

We worked with the Commerce Department extensively in the early years of the business and less now as we've gained experience. Ditmar Gorges gave you the example of when we targeted the Philippines, and we received word from the U.S. Commercial Service office at the embassy in Manila that the McDonald's franchiser there wanted to overhaul bathrooms in all the Manila restaurants. Somehow, the U.S. Commercial Service got wind of this, knew our product, and called us with the lead. Meetings were arranged for us, introductions were made, and it wasn't long before we had the contract.

Falcon Waterfree receives the E-Award from former Secretary of Commerce John Bryson.

Other benefits followed. The McDonald's put a sign over the urinals touting their environmental friendliness. The owner of a five-star hotel in Manila, who used that restroom one day, was so impressed that he ordered them installed in his hotel's public restrooms. And that wasn't all. The McDonald's chain asked if Falcon Waterfree could put the gold arches logo on the urinal ceramic bowl. We said, "Why not?" And soon male customers were asking if they could buy the golden arches waterless urinal at the counter along with their Big Macs. They couldn't, but the importance of word of mouth and the market intelligence capabilities of the U.S. Commercial Service were not lost on us.

We signed up with the U.S. Commercial Service office in Japan for long-term technical assistance that included research on building codes, meetings with government officials, and introductions to the best people to talk to in companies that could make suitable business partners. Companies in Asia and elsewhere in the world seem to respect the U.S. government presence in our meetings. You get the sense that they are on their best behavior.

A U.S. Commercial Service representative attended 24 meetings between Falcon Waterfree and a Japanese urinal manufacturer that became the leading suitor. In the end, a deal was signed, and Falcon Waterfree now has a strong foothold in this important market. The U.S. Commercial Service was invaluable to us. They gave us insight on the business culture and how the Japanese viewed the terms of the contract. They had unbelievable market intelligence. In market after market, they knew. No one else did. As Ditmar told you, we were particularly pleased when our Japanese partners told us later, "The Japanese government doesn't provide us this level of assistance. When we go to places like China, we are on our own. You Americans have the edge. You are lucky."

"... countries with free-trade agreements with the U.S. [can] enjoy the benefits of not paying duties and taxes for [our] product ..."

What were the other big lessons for the company in doing business around the world?

Adapting our product to new markets has been among the most useful lessons learned. Different cultures have different "bathroom cultures," and recognizing these differences was key to adapting the product. Urinals tend to be round in European countries and square in Asian countries. Also, different cultures clean toilets differently. Europeans use sponges and cloth wipes, but Japanese prefer to keep their distance from the cleaning surfaces and tend to use brushes. These differences are important when writing instruction manuals for use of the products. We also learned that different cultures have shorter time horizons for getting to know you and deciding to buy. In Europe and some Asian countries, this process can happen quickly. But other places take more time. In Japan, for example, it took Falcon Waterfree 5 years to make its first major sale. The other lesson we learned is that, even with a small team, you can accomplish great things. ⏀

Carlos Lemos
CEO, Ambient Technologies

Tell us a little bit about the history of your company, when it started, and what you produce.

We started our business in 1993. I worked for a very large consulting firm for many years—22 years. And then I decided to take my Brazilian heritage and live the American dream, which was running your own business. So I retired from the larger company and started my own company. We do geology, geophysics, drilling services. We support other companies that are looking to find information that's below the ground, whether it's groundwater related, whether it's construction related, whether it's engineering related, whether it is anything related with infrastructure issues, mining.

Is this expertise mainly in your head rather than any special equipment that you have developed yourself and that you use?

We use quite a bit of equipment. From the geophysics side, there's an awful lot of electronics. And most of these—this equipment is seismograph, electromagnetics, ground-penetrating radars. So we use pretty sophisticated pieces of equipment in our business. I would say we probably have invested at least over half a million dollars in equipment of that type. The other more bulky and bigger and meaner equipment is the drill rigs, made in Pennsylvania.

So you interpret the data that this equipment and technology produces.

Yes, we do. We present, like, profiles of the geological conditions. The project we're working on right now is the Panama Canal extension. So what we're doing is we're doing all the drilling underneath where the new set of locks is going to be, as the third set of locks is being built next to the existing locks. It will accommodate the much bigger ships. And it's a huge, huge, huge operation because it also involves a lot of retention basins because they're circulating the water instead of just simply discharging it to the ocean. So the construction is very big. We are drilling there because they found some geological faults. They're trying to study it, be sure that the design is appropriate to what we're finding. That's the kind of study we're doing. We do this both with the drill rig and the geophysics.

And the fault could suggest future earthquakes?

Yes, they've had earthquakes there. This particular fault isn't necessarily a recent fault. Part of the study is to determine whether the fault is recent or not. If it's a recent fault, of course there will be all kinds of concerns. If it is an old fault, then not so much.

Drilling at Valeza. Data from drilling reveals the safest places to dig.

And are there construction techniques that can take into account a fault and still go ahead with the digging and the building, regardless of the presence of the fault?

There are some design things that the structural engineers can do to accommodate that kind of movement—if it's really, really, really violent, you know—you saw what happened in Los Angeles and San Francisco. So you can design it to absorb quite a bit of the quake. But it's not foolproof. So what you do is you look at the risks of building and if it turns out that the signs are that it's extremely risky, then the design may change very significantly or may even be relocated. This is being done in conjunction with the existing lake—Gatun Lake—which is right there in the middle of it. That's how you really come across the Isthmus of Panama. You really go across the lake and you go down one side and up the other and out the other side.

You were honored recently in Washington, D.C., and at the White House for your activities in exporting from the U.S. to other countries. Can you tell us what was one of the main challenges you faced as a company and as the CEO in trying to enter the international marketplace?

The challenges can appear enormous when you're thinking as a small business. My first attempt to export was going to be to my native country. I spoke Portuguese and was born in Brazil. I felt comfortable there. But Brazil is so big and it's so challenging and so competitive that it didn't work out that well. It was great to reunite with family, but it wasn't very good for business. So I decided to pursue opportunities in countries where they weren't quite so big, and were comfortable working with smaller companies. So we started looking at countries in Central America. And you know, before we made the move into Central America, we had a pretty good idea what we thought was going to happen. And if it weren't for the Commerce Department, I could have never afforded doing that on my own, just on my own nickel. Let's put it this way now: the Department does charge something for finding customers for us, but it is for far less money than if I did it on my own. So it was very, very, very helpful. I mean, truly speaking, in 2008, when everything kind of collapsed, I looked at all my drilling rigs parked and I said, "What am I going to do with this?" Going international became a matter of necessity as much as just a whim. And then by that time I had gone overseas to look at the opportunities and saw Panama as an opportunity. Other countries at that time were looking at doing some other projects, including Colombia. I said, "We have to look at an international way to survive." So we took the leap of faith and went over there and took our equipment. And then, when the canal started, we had the equipment there and many people didn't. We were the first American company to work with the consortium that's building the canal.

What kinds of introductions were made so that they enabled you to be able to compete for that work?

What we did through the Department of Commerce is I was able to meet, number one, very important: the canal authority—the ACP—Autoridad del Canal de Panamá. And they were the people that were going to procure the work—now, not necessarily directly from us, but at least they knew that the work was coming, that they were going to need what we had. Actually, when the opportunity came for others, and they asked, "What company in Panama does this thing?" It was easy to say, "Well, we have these companies." So they helped us; introduced us to the consortiums. They had one or were bidding out for the opportunities. So that was fantastic—and that came through the Department of Commerce introduction. We also got introduced to the local engineering community, which was also very good. I met with the directors of several companies, contractors, and engineers. They told me what they expected and were actually very supportive. They said, "We welcome you because we're going to have more work than we can handle. So yeah—come on down and work with us." And they are very pro-American in Panama, I find. And they were very glad for us to have gone there.

What part of your annual revenue is from your international activities?

Right now, we are about 20 percent, maybe 25 percent, and it's growing. We were fortunate enough also that we had quite a bit of business in Florida related to sinkhole studies. So that kind of kept us going in Florida. And then the international was just building slowly, but building. We're being asked to go to Colombia now to work there as well. And that could further expand our revenues. So I'm looking for the international business to grow. And I wouldn't be surprised if in the next few years international is equal to U.S. business.

How many employees do you have now, and what sort of challenges do you face in scaling up to be able to serve this growing market?

Being small is not easy. It's difficult to get, for example, a simple thing like being able to find financing for a drill rig to take it overseas. If you go through a conventional bank, they don't like to see their assets outside the country. So it doesn't make any difference that I've just won a $2 million contract. The fact is that I can't buy the drill rig because the asset is going there. So that situation makes it very difficult because I have a very hard time finding financing for the tools that I need to do my job. And so that is a big issue that I'm confronted with. And hopefully with some of these new export promotion initiatives now, the funding might be a little bit easier to get or government funding guarantees that can help us do that sort of thing. Also, it's not so bad in Florida, but finding bilingual technical people is a challenge—people that have a degree in science, engineering, that are also bilingual and willing to go overseas for periods of time.

What advice do you have for U.S. businesspeople who aren't exporting now or only dabbling in it? What would you encourage them to do based on what you have learned in your own experience?

I really believe that one of the things they should do is really get involved with the local offices of the U.S. Department of Commerce Commercial Service, because that's what was successful for me. Also be prepared that there is a cost in getting started that is not going to be immediate gratification. Somewhere along the way you have to take a leap of faith and do it, and if it is well calculated enough you know that you're going to get returns for what you invested. Trying to go in and put a little money in and expecting to get big rewards very quickly just doesn't work.

What are the other gains and benefits from doing business outside your own country and culture?

It is the human factor of it all. It's the reward that you have by interacting with other cultures. It's the reward that you get to see that your employees are seeing beyond what's right here in front of their eyes, that they actually see now the world in a more global view than just right here. Those are the rewarding things that I see. It is rewarding to me to be able to make others see the U.S. for what we do—in a different light than many see it. And it makes you feel good.

Is Ambient a better company because of its exporting?

By far, by far it's a better company. I do believe that the employees are a little more proud that we are a global business than when we were just a local business. There's something about it that makes them more enthusiastic. And therefore, you know, the employees are the company. If they're feeling good and they feel proud, the company feels better. This is just, I think, human nature. And I do believe that the company's got a long way to go. It's an infinite job to train, and some things you can't train. So you have to find the right people that have it already in them, and sometimes I may hire a biologist to do a job that involves geology, but because of their attitude and their ability to deal with other cultures and deal with other people, they're by far a better employee. So I think in general it is very rewarding for everybody. And to me, of course, it's very rewarding because I see that happening. I love to see when the guys mature into the role of mini-ambassadors.

What other benefits have you realized by taking your company of 55 employees global?

Actually, what's happening is that the bigger companies now see us as a very good team member. Let's say they are a huge engineering firm and they have a project, let's say, in Suriname or in the Caribbean somewhere. And they say, "Well good, let's call Carlos because he has international experience," as if I've been everywhere in the world, when in reality I'm limited to only about four countries or so. But they say, "Call him because he's used to shipping rigs, moving people around, sending drill rigs. Can't get in touch with him? See if he's interested in going and working with us on these projects." So we sort of became a little bit of an international entity within the community of engineering—one of the few people who's willing to go. And that's even a bigger advantage because I'm getting calls from all the big companies. We got a call from a company in Texas that wants us to go to Honduras next month to do an environmental project at several gas stations. And that came because, I guess, the word gets spread around that we are willing to go. We're willing to deal with the headaches of dealing with customs. We're willing to deal with the inconveniences of the locals and all these other issues that quite frequently are not that bad. But that's OK, they can think that. It gives me more business. So we take advantage of that. We do things that nobody else wants to do. ◊

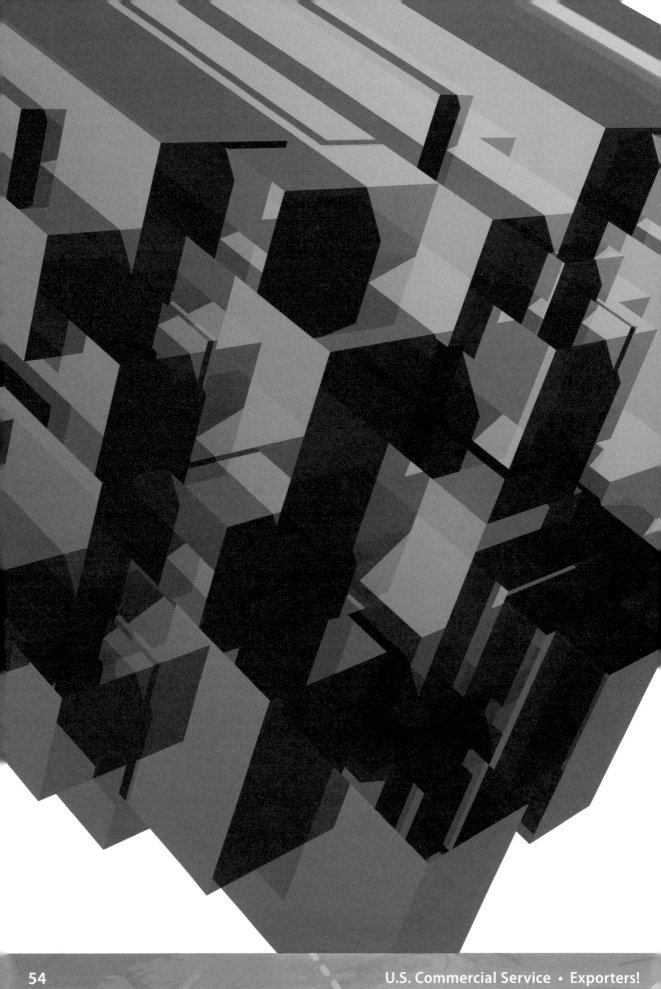

John H. Sohl III
CEO, Columbia Technologies

You're a specialty contractor and you use visualization, mapping, and tracking tools to do data collection analyses for soil pollution and groundwater. Can you tell us what all that means? What do you really do?

I'd be happy to do so. Basically, Columbia Technologies is involved in the mapping of underground pollution from major manufacturing facilities, oil terminals, depots, pipelines, and military bases. And so what we do is deploy sensor technologies through fairly smart people and smart tools out around the globe, to take a look underneath these facilities and track the leakage and the migration of pollutions. This allows the customers to make a decision on risk assessment, disposition of the property, and proper cleanup actions.

How did you get into this business and when did it all start?

I got into this business probably about 15 years ago. I served in the U.S. Navy and was working with these types of issues on facilities within the navy and then migrated out of the navy and into this commercial field doing the same sort of thing. I was always intrigued with the application of sensors and three-dimensional mapping of components, and what we brought into the industry was that approach.

And then a lot of the business was done locally or domestically—what got you involved in the wider world?

I think, as everyone recognizes, the flow of people, capital, and businesses is fairly fluid in today's world. So many of our clients are global industries that have footprints both in the U.S. and elsewhere in North America as well as the globe. Once we established a good working relationship and reputation with those firms, they sought to bring us into other parts of the globe. We first migrated to Canada and performed services up there, and second, went down to Mexico and performed the same types of services, and additional services. Those are the first two exports in terms of direct boots on the ground, so to speak, of sensors and folks.

Where are you now? How many countries?

We have advanced work going into Latin America. Brazil, Argentina, and Colombia. And that work came as a major benefit of working with the U.S. Commerce Department, which offers an exposition called Trade Winds. Trade Winds occurs in a different country or region of the world every year and connects us with personnel at U.S. embassies. These events and meetings give us the ability to evaluate the markets on a case-by-case basis and then pick the best targets of opportunity. And so we've gone in there to identify service partners, professional services, import/export laws and things of that sort. We're planning business into Brazil and Argentina in the near future.

So Mexico, Canada, Brazil, Argentina— where else?

We've made visits to Colombia and we're in discussions with Peru.

Are you looking to expand beyond Latin America?

Again, I think globalization drives a lot of the decision making, and then we have to basically do it on a resource—what's our capacity as a small business to move into markets? So we're focusing on Latin America at this point in time based on the customer base and their range—and the business deals that we can put together in those markets. I would say the area of interest for us is to move into Asia and a much more complex world. And we're evaluating that opportunity in the coming months.

Smart people and tools assist in tracking underground pollution.

And how many of you are there?

We've added 2 to 3 people, which for us is about a 20 to 30 percent growth. So we started at about 10 people, we're up to 12 to 13 now. We actually are actively recruiting folks. When the business starts in Brazil, we'll probably have to double the size of the staff in order to execute that work. International means a lot to us.

What's the most interesting experience that you've had in traveling around Latin America doing this sort of work? Anything out of the ordinary or surprising?

How well we are welcomed into these countries to bring in our knowledge or expertise and work with local people, alongside them, has been a very positive surprise for us. Having had a career in the navy you certainly spend a lot of time visiting foreign countries. So that wasn't really a pushback for me personally or many of our staff.

But I think what was really a very pleasant surprise was how eager people were to help us move into those countries and bring the services in there, because a lot of the technologies the U.S. companies have are unique in some of these other locations. I was really welcomed with open arms to come down there.

So the U.S. brand does have cachet outside of the U.S.?

The U.S. brand does have cachet. It's related to the expertise, the experience, the technologies. I think many of the purchase decisions are made based on the fact that we are bringing to our customers quite a valued proposition.

Regarding things like regulations in other countries, payment, all of the export process things that have to be dealt with, have you found any of that to be challenging?

Each country has its way of doing business. Each country has its own set of rules, regulations, import and export requirements. Again, challenging, but in a lot of ways not any more so than it is in the U.S. today. Our government here and around the world helps us work through that because we're connected up with potential service partners that can help us work through the legal, import, and export issues.

It doesn't mean each one isn't a little bit of a surprise, but we have someone to lean on and help us through that process. We heard a lot of horror stories about payment terms and security of equipment and that sort of thing. I can say, so far, our experience has been nothing but positive. We had very, very few issues with payment terms, and certainly had some slowdowns in moving equipment and things into various countries; but nothing that we didn't really anticipate, I guess.

How do you handle payment? Letters of credit?

We actually rely on our customers for direct payment. We lean a lot on the customer to help us with a down payment to help us support the transport of equipment. There are also several members of banking associations here in the U.S. that are strongly supportive of the export requirements. We haven't yet moved up to the letter of credit level, as we are able to execute payment terms with our customers.

You mentioned that the U.S. government, through the Department of Commerce, the U.S. Commercial Service, has been very helpful to your company. Can you think of one particular example of something very helpful that was provided to you and actually turned into real, concrete business?

Oh, absolutely. Take Mexico. We went down to the Trade Winds conference and were introduced again to legal, accounting, and import and export organizations, as well as U.S. Embassy staff. I made several visits to the embassy to gain introduction to other members of the community. And that visit led to very specific additional work. They can open doors and introduce you to folks that are connected to business.

What other advice would you have for the U.S. businessperson who is maybe contemplating exporting but hasn't done it yet—or maybe did a few years ago—did it once or twice, business picked up for them here in the domestic market, and then they decided not to do it anymore?

Each business and each business owner has to make their own decisions about where their products and services have a market and what's happening. The first thing you need to do is look at things on a global scale. And I think you can learn that from the investment community, that the flow of the goods and services is truly global, it's not U.S. based. Probably the primary piece of advice is: Don't feel like you have to do it alone. Sit down with your local government representative, lay out a strategy, think through the strategy. Don't just try to go execute without thinking through all the pieces of the puzzle. Use the resources. Make more than one visit. You can do it very systematically, in a very coordinated planning mode. You don't have to do it as a fire drill.

The world would seem to have an insatiable appetite and need for the kind of services that you offer, given the condition of groundwater and all kinds of other waste that has been disposed of underground. It seems like this is a pretty good business to be in.

It does have a global appeal. The third piece of advice to the U.S. business owner, and particularly someone in the environmental industry, is to evaluate the receptiveness or the willingness or the readiness of a particular country to focus on their environmental issues, among other things. I mean, in obvious cases of unrest, you know, they're really not worried about the environmental issues at that point in time. But countries that have gone through and developed well-established property rights rules of law are enticing. They all need to make decisions about their property, real estate, and how to properly care for that. And so, yes—in that context, environmental is a very strong component. And it's very enticing to us and has been fruitful to this point.

Do you face major competition around the world?

I think an important point for any U.S. businessperson is that your primary competition is most likely a foreign competitor. And it wasn't all invented in the U.S. So, yes, there is strong competition from Europe, strong competition from some of the Asian countries, and from Australia. We need to understand that it's not just a U.S. market out there. It's very much a global market.

In being out there against this competition, pitting yourself against them, presumably learning from them, what has your company learned as a result of these experiences? What has it done for you?

I think we've just had validation of our ideas and basically the operating mission of our company, which is its execution. If you do your job well and provide a good value for a fair price, you're going to ... you're going to succeed in these countries and with these companies. It's still all about execution. You can't fake it. So if you're going to be in a country and executing in that country, you need to go ready to do the job and do it right.

Is there training or follow-up service after the sale?

Our strategy is that once we make the decision to make the export and entry into a country, we're going to stay. We go to build long-term relationships, both with our customers and with our partners. We're not there on a just-drop-in-and-do-some-work-and-leave kind of thing. Yes, there are a lot of ongoing client relationships that are important, both specifically for our client and also the business community. In other words, you have to go at it with a long-term perspective. ⊘

Patrick Dickey
Vice President, International Marketing, Solatube

What's a Solatube?

We are a San Diego-based maker of tubular skylights. But these aren't ordinary skylights. They employ patented technologies that bring more natural light in, and they come with optional kits that convert the skylight into a light fixture as the natural light fades or into a ventilator for kitchen and bathroom use. As the price of electricity increases, skylights for both home and commercial use save money and are good for the environment.

Solatube was founded in Australia in 1991. Its owners decamped for California to be closer to the U.S. domestic market and to Europe and Latin America. In the old days, we pushed out products with North America on the brain. Now we're thinking globally. North America will continue to pay most of the bills, but if we aren't competing in India, one day India will be competing with us in our home market. There is instant revenue from North America.

We learned that in North America 75 percent of our sales are residential; in foreign markets it's 98 percent commercial—all because of higher energy costs. So this tells us what to make, how to sell, and ultimately there will be demand for our product for a long time. Return on investment for our products in Asia is 4 years versus 25 years in North America.

Why don't more U.S. companies export?

Companies don't export because it appears daunting. "India? Are you kidding me? I don't want to lose control." For our company, when we see possibilities we don't hesitate. There is a cost—time, commitment, money. Don't do it halfway. Jump in with both feet. Be ready to take some hits. Once the sales start, it rolls in quickly and is exciting.

What's the extent of your international portfolio?

We are in 70 countries now. International sales currently account for 15 to 18 percent of total sales but are growing faster than North American sales. International is a bright spot. Asia is growing fast, and we now have 20 distributors in China.

What about your intellectual property?

Our product is simple and doesn't lend itself to IP protection. We've been in China for 4 years, based in Shanghai: Solatube China. We pulled our manufacturing back from China even though we had anticipated supplying the rest of the world from there. The cost savings never materialized because of wage increases, and we had a hard time controlling the operation, though quality didn't suffer. We were making bits there, while shipping the main parts from the U.S. We will always manufacture in the U.S. We're proud to say "Made in the U.S.," and foreign buyers like that. It's more expensive to make it here, but it's better to do it here. Many end users don't like the "Made in China" label.

Are you a better business because of your international footprint?

No question. Exporting has made Solatube's domestic business stronger. Experience in Europe and elsewhere in the world has turned us into something of a thought leader in our U.S. business dealings. Environmental practices in commercial buildings are sometimes more advanced in Europe than in the U.S. Solatube has brought those ideas back to the U.S. and had them adopted by our U.S. customers. It gives us a competitive advantage. Also, the U.S. companies we do work for overseas are eager to use us here in the U.S. The international work gives us credibility.

You work mainly with overseas distributors?

Yes. As a small company, we can't be experts in every market. We're not that naive to think we can do it all. We need to find entrepreneurial folks overseas who can find the people working on the roofs and who influence the purchasing decisions. We need national distributors with business backgrounds who can set up everything for us. At first, Solatube was mostly passive in its outreach, meeting potential distributors at trade shows or evaluating prospects who contacted Solatube through the Web or by phone. Results were very mixed, and the company spent more time on unfocused searching than on selling and growing the business. So Solatube approached the U.S. Commercial Service in San Diego. We did things the hard way for a number of years until we met the U.S. Commercial Service. We wished we had met them before. Trade Specialist Julia Rauner Guerrero entered the picture as Solatube set its sights on France. With help from her colleague Eva Prevost, in Marseille, Guerrero identified a number of master distributor prospects, including one who had seen Solatube promoted on the U.S. Commercial Service website in France. In the end, Solatube chose this distributor to represent the product line. Everything was wrapped up in less than 6 months, and orders were placed for $100,000 worth of product.

What have been the big lessons learned by your company?

Solatube's number one lesson learned was that small companies can expand internationally, gain significant new sales, and add jobs. Don't try to do it all yourself. It's easy to get overextended and to waste valuable time. There is a lot of excellent free and low-cost help out there, including that of the U.S. government and its partners. In the case of France, our Commercial Service contact there served as a filter for us. The French distributor would talk to Eva (at the U.S. Embassy in Paris) as both our representative there and as a representative of the U.S. government, and she would interpret things for us. There was a French-to-French thing going there that worked out great for us.

The most important thing you can do is to find good distributors in your target markets. You can spend lots of time and money finding them on your own, but let the government do it for you. This is their niche, and they're the best at it.

Diversifying economic risks really does work. When it's sunny in some of our markets, it's snowing in others. When business is down in the States, it's up somewhere else. Our overseas sales have been growing 25 percent a year for the past 6 years. Our international success has improved our acquisition profile. Not that we're looking to sell, but if we ever are in the future we'll be worth a lot more because of the international dimension of our business.

Navigating cultural issues with distributors can be a challenge. Don't be reluctant to ask for help. In one instance, after we agreed on a deal, we sent a contract to a distributor unsigned by us. The distributor was very upset, believing we didn't trust him. This would be unthinkable in his culture. There was no legal risk for us to sign it, so the reason we didn't was probably cultural. Knowing how not to unintentionally give offense is an important and easily learnable business skill.

Another lesson is don't hesitate to pursue multiple markets simultaneously. My boss thought I was crazy for pursuing multiple markets. "You'll only do it halfway," he warned me. I said to him, "We're not alone. We have an extension of the company working for us. It's the U.S. government in these markets. They've already helped us." He couldn't believe what we accomplished in 18 months. Distributors may not have talked to me without the U.S. government connection. Now I'm confident in targeting at the same time Egypt, Nigeria, Sri Lanka, Bangladesh, and Morocco. The other thing is to pick distributors with care. Yes, the U.S. government will help. But when we meet the prospective distributors we insist that they devote resources to building our business. They have to demonstrate their ability to get meetings with connections with multinational companies working in India or wherever we want to do business.

We don't hesitate to go into the international market. We always go 100 percent. Go hard, or go home. It's intimidating until you see the possibilities. ∅

Shane Cooper
President, DeFeet International

What do you make, and how did DeFeet start? Where did you get the idea?

My wife and I were bike racers back in the early 1990s. In the summertime she was supplementing her income by racing bikes as an amateur and I was spending her supplemental income as an amateur on my bike racing. My father was a sock-knitting-machine technician and sold the parts. So I grew up in the sock industry. I was a cyclist. I studied electronics engineering and am somewhat of a salesman. One day, I decided to make socks to pay for my racing. It just kind of happened from there. We made the world's best sock for cycling and that was 20 years ago. We have since branched out into running and skiing and to 35 countries worldwide.

Is that a pair of your socks on your feet?

Absolutely. This is the Peloton, made of merino wool. If you notice, there's a group of cyclists. The yellow jersey's right there. "Peloton" is a group of cyclists.

What was your biggest challenge in going international? You had this great background and created the product. But very few U.S. businesses go outside the U.S. looking for customers.

It happened by chance. We created a product that world-class cyclists were taking over to Europe. And we had this product on their feet. So there was a desire for the customer before we had international distribution. Our brand grew from there. Cycling in Europe is tremendous in size, similar to American baseball and football. I was struggling myself, not being a true businessman. Then I met this wonderful man, Lynn Moretz, who came into our company and became my mentor and helped us capitalize on this desire that we had created as a brand into a real business. So Lynn was able to take it into these countries and give structure behind the madness that I had created.

What was the challenge in going from a product that was transported by your U.S. customers and introduced to potential international buyers to where it really became a process and a strategy?

Process and strategy, pricing structures, the advent of the Internet, and what was going to play there and how it was going to actually work and these international customers over the course of the last 20 years were coming to our website, finding the product and going, "Where can I get it?" They would see it on the best riders in the world, from Tom Boonen and Mark Cavendish back to Paolo Bettini. They're asking where they could get it. I was too busy paying attention to R&D and the product to really focus on that. Then Lynn came in and provided that structure to actually make it happen.

Among all those different things—the pricing and selecting the best possible distributors—what in your mind was the biggest challenge that you overcame?

Unfortunately the year that my collaborator came to DeFeet, we burned down. We lost everything we had—2001, October, right after 9/11. We lost it all. And so we had 9 months of no production. That was our biggest challenge to get over. By the time we got over it, we had a new building and Lynn was able to come in and structure this system on the rebuild to get products into the hands of the international distributors to keep continue growing it.

> *"If we didn't have our international business, gosh, I don't think we would have made it."*

How did you rebuild? That would be a crushing thing to happen for most people. How did you manage to rise from the ashes, as it were?

I would like to say that I cut my hair off and used that to rebuild the building. But I think the hair came off in the process somewhere. We had insurance that covered the building, the equipment and the contents. And then we had insurance for business loss, income loss, which turned into a court battle for 3 years. When we finally got the check, we had to pay taxes out of that money because it's business income. So for the first 9 years of our business, we were profitable every year and growing organically. The banks loved us—or the banks hated us because we actually paid the loans off too early. We had 7 years where we made no money after the fire. We became profitable again and started winning the business back. Keep this in mind. It's 2008. We're profitable that year just in time for the worst economic downturn in world history that we know about, other than the Depression. The fortunate thing is that these bicycles were being pulled out of the garage and people were putting tires on them and commuting. It made the bicycle shops flush with cash. The dollar was going crazy with the euro. So all of a sudden, after 7 years of struggling, we made it through. And now, we're 4 years in with profits again.

Did your international expansion save you?

If we didn't have our international business, gosh, I don't think we would have made it.

So you and your wife are pretty persistent. Do you think that persistence is a useful skill to have in the international marketplace?

I think so. I think persistence is something that you have to have to be in business in any country. In my opinion, it may come from the bike racing that we did that hardened us and toughened us up. We're not quitters. We could have shut our plant down and moved it to Asia and had socks made over there. But we decided to stay put. We never missed a pay period with our employees. We buy local yarn and boxes. So even though we're only 38 employees now, the benefit is pretty widespread when we buy locally.

Why not outsource to China? Wouldn't it be cheaper in the long run?

Cheaper—that's a good word. I prefer the word "value." Why we prefer to use that word "value" is for long-lasting goodness, affordable price, and a sock that's going to last 10 years. I don't like the homogenization of other sock brands making their product in the same plant that I'm making mine in and all of a sudden my trade secrets are gone. I don't like the environmental issue. I don't like the lead in the toys, the drywall issues with radioactive materials, and the lunch boxes with the toxic waste in them. We have a very environmentally friendly facility in the U.S. We make our socks out of recycled water bottles. But our building is comfortable for our employees. It's air conditioned; it's well lit. It's very clean and very safe. You hit a nerve there. So "American made" to me is control. It's American jobs. It's quality, and mostly it's value. Value is not the word you used earlier—cheap. "Cheap" means that it's cheap and you are not going to get the same value that you get when you pay for the better product.

How do you make socks out of recycled water bottles?

Our suppliers take some of the hundred million plastic water bottles that are thrown away every day in North America. They crunch them up, grind them up, melt them, turn them into pellets, and then they extrude them in a big vat into Coolmax material. That is a wicking polyester. That is what we use.

And when did the U.S. Department of Commerce and the U.S. Commercial Service in particular, come into the story?

Any time we have a question about a tariff, or when we're dealing with Australia and we're not sure what to do, or a new free-trade agreement, or some new idea comes up, we call the U.S. Commercial Service office in Charlotte. Then there are international textile agreements and an understanding of how the sock is structured, with what material, and where the fibers come from and what category it fits in. The Commerce guys have been a great help there. You've got to remember, I was a dumb bike racer, a bad one at that. I wasn't a businessman. So having the U.S. Commercial Service nearby and the offices at the embassies in the countries where we want to set up distributors, and to help the brand that my wife and I created—and she's the brains behind the organization—to have that U.S. Commercial Service office there to help us is all very supportive.

How many countries do you sell to and what percentage of revenues is from international sales?

We are in 35 countries, and I believe about 25 percent of our revenue is international.

Do you think DeFeet is a better company now as a result of your international exploits? What have you learned that you've applied?

It's interesting because DeFeet is so much more of a brand in Europe than in America because the sport we chose to really specialize in—even though we make running and ski socks—is our big one, cycling. Our international distributors made this happen. But it's the customers we developed—

Shane Cooper (right) in Europe with members of his marketing team.

developed the brand that they had a passion for. Unlike other sock companies, there are traditional companies that make the product and then try to sell the product. We get input from the word's best riders. Paolo Bettini, the Italian national champion, world champion, Olympic champion—sat down with me and we had a translator on what he needed in a sock. We then listened to him and made that sock available to the public. So we used the world's best cyclists to develop the sock, and then we took it to their fan base. If you go watch the Tour de France or the Giro d'Italia, that are sponsored events, there are five teams competing that are using our product. So those guys are defining the product that Americans will be wearing in the next 5 years.

Is it a trade secret or can you tell us what he told you?

That is a trade secret.

Are there cultural differences in designing and selling your socks?

There are cultural differences in color. There are cultural differences in what you can actually say on a sock. You know, you can say some word that might mean something in one country. Another country, it might mean something bad. So we have to be very careful, even though we're an edgy company. We do a lot of flag colors. We'll do a lot of tricolor socks for the Italians, with their Italian national flags. And flags are a funny thing because my Texas rep once told me back about 15 years ago, he said, make me a sock with a Texas flag on it. I said, "Yeah, like that's going to sell." It's been our number one selling sock for 6 years. So even in America, you know, with the capacities that we have, the logo can really be very regional. So a logo about the Giro d'Italia right now will sell really well in Italy. It will sell good around the world, but much better in Italy. The Tour de France, there's going to be a whole different color way. You know, yellow is going to be the color instead of the pink. Pink is the color of the Giro d'Italia winner's jersey.

Based on your experience and what you've learned over the last years, what would you advise other companies considering starting or expanding export sales?

Look at yourself and figure out what your strengths and weaknesses are. If your strengths are that you can do the international part of your business yourself, then do it. If not, hire a mentor. Find a mentor that will help you, the one that's been there and done that. Use every available government agency's help as well to really make your life a lot easier. If you don't have the skills or time to do the international, hire someone who can do it. ✐

Kimberly Brown
Owner, Amethyst Technologies

Tell us a little bit about what you do and a little about your company.

Amethyst Technologies is the company I founded 4 years ago. We provide services to support drug control, global health, vaccine development, and clinical trials in the U.S. and in Africa. Primarily, we provide quality control services, we develop training programs, we set up laboratories, and we provide assistance for research and development. So what we do varies. We provide engineering functions, quality functions, software development, and research and development.

What countries are you currently working in?

We work, of course, in the U.S. We also work in Tanzania and Kenya. We have a DOD contract that has a scope of work to develop quality control programs for malaria.

What other agencies have you worked with, or governments, in getting business in these countries in Africa?

Right now all of our work in Africa is through the Department of Defense. We are preparing for a new contract with a large commercial company.

So it sounds like the U.S. government is a good entry point for certain kinds of companies to get into the international marketplace.

I definitely agree with that statement. It was our first prime contract. And we had different tasks. And our last task was the Tanzania-scope project. So as a small business, we were just trying to do business in Maryland. And we were given the opportunity to provide services to support the U.S. Army in Tanzania and Kenya. That's really the only reason why we are in Africa now and pursuing the opportunities.

Are you interested in pursuing additional opportunities in Africa from sources other than the U.S. government, such as an African government?

We are currently actively pursuing opportunities in about five countries, and just won a contract in Zambia. Most of those opportunities right now are with foreign governments. We also have been talking to the large . . . some of the large Non-Governmental Organizations (NGOs). Because our work supports global health initiatives, we have value-added resources to assist with the President's Malaria Initiative, with the Global Health Initiative.

> "The time involved—again, as a small business—you're going to need somebody who knows how to do business in that country."

It must be a wonderful feeling to get up every day realizing that you're contributing to saving lives and improving the lives of potentially millions of people.

Definitely. It makes it all worthwhile. It's an added bonus to doing business when you're doing something that is very beneficial, very needed, and it will change lives. Small things can make a very large difference.

How did you came into contact with the U.S. Commercial Service in Baltimore?

I attended an event and met someone from the U.S. Commercial Service. And that's really how I came in contact with the organization. I hadn't heard anything about it. I didn't know that they had resources to help businesses like Amethyst Technologies.

> " . . . do your homework. Use the U.S. Commercial Service to research any country that you are thinking about doing business in."

What did you hear specifically at that meeting that piqued your curiosity?

I heard that they can help us identify partners. They can also assist us with identifying what countries we can do business with and what type of business we can do. So as a small business, for me, that levels the playing field, because large businesses which are doing business overseas, they have a whole department that's dedicated to providing these types of services. And I found out that the U.S. government will provide those services for me and my company.

Did you have mixed feelings at the beginning about the government and contacting them and working with them?

I've always had very positive results and had great assistance from government agencies. My company, we are an SBA company. So I never had any hesitance to contact them and am always seeking opportunities to contact government agencies to get resources, especially with doing business overseas.

> "As a small business we need to do what the large businesses are doing."

Do you think that's a competitive advantage for U.S. businesses to know about the government services available and take full use of their services?

Definitely. As a small business, and even large businesses now, you need to take advantage of any information that you can receive that is appropriate, that is correct, and is at no or little cost.

In dealing in Africa and with a different culture, have you or your company had to make certain, you know, changes, or develop a different mind-set in order to effectively interact with people?

We really haven't had many problems in interacting, other than language barriers. In Tanzania, everything is in Swahili. So we had to have all our documents translated to Swahili and we hire interpreters. But other than that, it's really been a very smooth transition, especially in health care. That's a global language. And everyone understands malaria. And that's what we're doing in Tanzania.

What else are you considering now about positioning your company to do more of this kind of work?

Definitely diversifying, listening to the large businesses like GE. I attended an event a few years ago, and the CEO of GE talked about going global. And that always stuck with me, that as a small business we need to do what the large businesses are doing. Creating jobs in the U.S., doing work overseas is our model. So we have been aligning ourselves with partners: public and private partnerships; that's really what we're focusing on now.

Do you have a person that does that full time, or is that you?

That's all of us. Primarily it's me, but the persons who are working in Africa, they will often identify opportunities.

And how many employees do you have?

We have 23 employees.

Who does what?

We're half engineers. We have a software developer with a background in artificial intelligence. We have an archivist. We have a technical writer. We have a whole group of quality assurance professionals. And then we have office management.

As a nonengineer—what do engineers contribute to the finding of cures for malaria and other kinds of diseases?

We set up laboratories. One of the primary things we do on the engineering side is ensure FDA (Food and Drug Administration) compliance for equipment, we develop software, we procure—we get specs for clean rooms, laboratories. So those are some of the things that we're doing and pursuing overseas, setting up World Health Organization–compliant laboratories for drug testing, developing standards for education, for health care, for transportation and agriculture. So as engineers, we offer something very unique and beneficial to global health.

> *"Creating jobs in the U.S., doing work overseas is our model."*

As you know, there's a lot of fear and paranoia, paralysis even, when it comes to thinking about selling something to somebody in a different country. And what would you say now to the fearful, based on your experience?

Definitely do your homework. Use the U.S. Commercial Service to research any country that you are thinking about doing business in. Find out what the markets are, what are the positives, what are the negatives. And look for in-country partners. Both of those things are resources that the U.S. Commercial Service specializes in helping businesses with. In my first meeting with the U.S. Commercial Service, I was told that I needed to find a partner. Before that, I thought that Amethyst could just go in and get a contract or look for opportunities. So they really opened my eyes to finding a partner. And that is very important, because in many countries a U.S. company can't own a business; you can't be the primary majority owner. So you will need an in-country partner just to do business, because every country is so different.

The time involved—again, as a small business—you're going to need somebody who knows how to do business in that country. And then the connections—even in the U.S.—you have to know people. So it's great advice that I received from the U.S. Commercial Service that is really making a difference in our pursuit of opportunities abroad. ✎

Terry Dittrich
International Sales Manager,
Spancrete Machinery Corporation (SMC)

How did Spancrete get started?

Spancrete Global Services Incorporated, a division of the Spancrete Group, employs 45 people in its Waukesha, Wisconsin, production facility. The firm, founded by Henry Nagy, manufactured the first precast hollow-core slabs in North America in 1952. SMC sells its equipment worldwide under license agreements and direct sales. We try to be in every market where there is lots of construction and money to pay for it. In the last 5 years we've entered India, the Middle East, Kazakhstan and, more recently, the Russian Far East. Libya is up next. We're also interested in Brazil, but the government there imposes import taxes of more than 60 percent on our products. I'm hopeful that when the policy people find that they can't grow the economy by excluding needed technology, they'll reduce these taxes.

What's going on in these developing markets?

We're building two plants in Yakutsk in the Russian Far East. The region is one of the coldest places on the planet. It gets to 45 degrees below zero or colder in the winter. I met the Yakutian customer at a trade show in St. Petersburg, Russia. He invited me to Yakutsk. I got on a plane after the show and flew there. In Blagoveshchensk, what used to be known as the Jewish Autonomous Region—but I don't think it was Jewish or autonomous, they are building a new space center. They're rocking and rolling.

Kazakhstan is starting a building boom with oil money. I see a lot of work ahead with housing, new schools, office buildings. A lot of the kids there go to college in the UK and the U.S. They speak excellent English, and when you go there to talk to the companies involved in the building projects, it's like working with a U.S. company. The guy who is buying our plants owns a building supply company, a construction company, and a mortgage company. Holy cow! He then hires foreign architects, including U.S. ones, to design the buildings.

In Saudi Arabia, they have plans to build tons of universities and schools. Forty percent of the population is under 30 years of age. They are also going to start public housing projects in the big cities, because a big percentage of the population is not wealthy and the housing stock is in bad shape.

Not many people, especially Americans, would jump on a plane to a place called Yakutsk.

The mentality of Americans is to be satisfied with the North American market. It's just plain shortsighted. Their competitors in the other markets are making money, and sooner or later they'll be here, more competitive because of their experience in some of these developing markets. Even in a downturn in the domestic economy, getting U.S. companies to go overseas is like pulling teeth. Saudi Arabia has billions of dollars to spend on construction projects. We're not there. The Chinese are there. We're sitting in North America wondering, "Is it safe over there?"

The state and federal governments need to browbeat our companies. "How can you not be there?" I'm bringing U.S. companies to construction trade shows in the Middle East. They are our suppliers. All of them made sales. I contacted over 100 companies, but only eight committed to coming. Now they're believers. In contrast, the Germans will bring 300 of their companies to a trade show—lawyers, finance guys. The German prime minister will fly in to cut the ribbon to open the show. We don't have that kind of horsepower going for us. Embassies are, in some markets, backed up with requests for business matchmaking. I'm told that it will take many months to find me additional buyer prospects in Kazakhstan. The states are back in the trade promotion business. They have grants and do trade missions. But most of them shut their trade offices years ago, so it's the embassy that is asked to do all the work.

What's happened with China and what were the challenges there?

We entered China in the late 1980s. We wanted to incorporate licensing agreements, but the Chinese government forbade such arrangements. So we opted to sell the machinery outright. Nevertheless, our hollow-core machines were the first foreign equipment of that type sold in China. The early years were challenging. Our customers were state-owned enterprises, and the Chinese government encouraged them to expand into the precast construction business, despite their limited knowledge of that sector. Those companies started by producing floor slabs, our most basic product, but local architects and engineers had limited experience with precast products of this type. Even in a state-controlled economic system, companies need effective marketing to generate sales. To better support the companies, we began assisting with seminars for these state-owned enterprises and the construction community in general.

Terry in China with customers.

Our next achievement was to establish the China Spancrete Association, probably the first organization of its kind. The association is a nonprofit support organization for our Chinese customers, assisting them in technical, production, and marketing procedures. At first, the Chinese didn't understand the concept of a professional association. They said, "Why should we pay dues to belong to something like this? Why should we cooperate with people outside of our own enterprise?" It's not how they operated. Now they can see the value and continue to expand the association's efforts.

Working through the association, we pooled the existing knowledge for the benefit of all members. The association tackled the lack of codes and standards, making recommendations on matters like the loads that floors can safely carry and conducting research on seismic and fire-safety issues. Ultimately our company, with the association, achieved the registration of Spancrete-China products in the national building and design code. Business processes are changing rapidly in China, and competitors are getting more aggressive. Also, the economic boom has moved south and west of where it started, creating more opportunities and challenges. Today, China is doing OK business-wise. The long-awaited and sweeping new building codes have taken ages to approve. The codes should be released soon, at which time another boom is possible, and we're ready for it.

Is China alone in adopting new building standards?

Not at all. Around the world, we see construction design and standards improving. The engineering is becoming more skilled. The public is demanding safer construction. Many developing countries are emulating Western and U.S. standards, which are best implemented using U.S. equipment. Markets are demanding faster, cheaper, sustainable. All are strong suits of U.S. suppliers.

You mentioned that the U.S. government should "browbeat" U.S. companies by asking why they are not seeking business in these markets. What other help has the government provided?

Recently, I used the U.S. Commercial Service's Gold Key Service and Single Company Promotion program in seven Chinese cities. The U.S. Commercial Service identified local companies interested in purchasing our equipment systems and coordinated meetings with key government officials. They've been helpful in India, Russia, and Kazakhstan, though we've run into capacity issues in Kazakhstan. All in all, the service is amazing.

Has the company's international experience made Spancrete a better company?

The experience in international markets has made me a more effective professional and the company more competitive. There's just no doubt that selling overseas has made us a more effective exporter and our products more competitive. We simplified our product right down to our software so everything is easier to operate, no matter what the conditions or the language spoken. Our key personnel have grown from the international experience, and we continuously bring ideas back home and apply them throughout the company. Competition is tough in these markets, but that's where the opportunities are. Exporting is no longer just an option, and America's export future lies in these markets. ✐

Yoshino Nakajima
Vice President, International Market Development, Home Instead Senior Care

How did this business get started?

Home Instead Senior Care, a franchise service company based in Omaha, Nebraska, is a worldwide leader of nonmedical care for senior citizens who choose to remain at home but require personal care, companionship, meal preparation, light housekeeping, medicine reminders, and help with errands and shopping. The company was started in 1994 by Paul Hogan.

How did he get the idea?

Paul had a grandma who was 88 and very frail. She had 15 children and 55 grandchildren. The family did a schedule for round-the-clock care, but there were still gaps. This was the challenge, so in his twenties Paul started a business based on the needs of his grandmother. That was 1994, in Omaha. Home Instead Senior Care expanded to nearly 100 domestic franchise offices in just 3 years, making it one of the fastest growing franchise companies in the U.S. Having found success in the domestic market, the company began receiving inquiries about taking its franchise concept international. In 2012 we opened our thousandth franchise. There are 40 of us at the HQ, and we expect to add 30 more next year. Revenues hit $1 billion in 2011. The company's international success has contributed to our growth, with the development of a new technology department in its international division that has created new jobs at the company's headquarters in Omaha. The new department saves the company time and helps ensure the quality of services.

How did you get into such a good and socially useful business?

I was living in Poland, where I owned a Blimpie franchise with two other people. It was pretty successful, given that Poland wasn't a very open economy then. My parents were in Japan and I was feeling guilty. I saw an article about Paul and called him. I told him that there is a need for his concept in Japan and elsewhere, and if he hired me I'd take his business global. There was complete silence on the phone. He thought about it for awhile, then he hired me. I sold my share in the Blimpie franchise.

I was very impressed with Home Instead Senior Care's brand promise of reliable, responsive, and trained caregivers who create an atmosphere of trust for clients and their families. With the world's aging population increasing, families like mine, worldwide, are in need of these meaningful services for their aging relatives.

Aging populations create service opportunities worldwide.

Japan can be a tough market, especially if it's your first beyond North America. How did your entry into Japan go?

Our concept of companionship for senior citizens did not exist in Japan. We had to focus on educating a community on the expanded meaning of companionship for the elderly, and how our services could help families. We held a press conference to introduce the new word *konpanyanshippu* to the Japanese community. Together with market research and additional publicity we were able to initiate an effective market entry strategy. Japan is the world's second-largest economy, and its family-oriented culture and aging population showed strong potential for introducing our services. We signed a master franchising agreement with Japan's leading service-oriented provider that has generated more than 100 Japanese franchise offices. Interestingly, the new Japanese word is in common use today.

What happened after Japan?

Having succeeded in Japan, we wanted to enter the Western European market, but faced new hurdles. In Japan, the public was not concerned with the price so much as the type of service, whereas in Europe, price was a major concern. Instead of having to introduce the concept of companionship, we had to reclassify our services into three levels as a way for clients to save money.

> "Caring for the elderly is one of the biggest social challenges of our time."

In Portugal, two men approached us about opening a franchise in Lisbon. They had been unable to find the right level of care for their ailing parents without having to pay for unneeded services, and they wanted to help other families with similar problems. The men signed an agreement with the company in 2003 to start their own franchise. This began the company's three-tiered marketing strategy for Europe.

Have the franchisees suffered during the recession in Europe?

Interestingly, no. Both Portugal and Spain are doing well. The sovereign debt problems there have not negatively affected the demand for care for seniors.

> "The Web is very important for reaching the adult children. We pay to be in the top 10 listings of the important search engines."

Where else have you expanded?

After Japan and Portugal the company has signed master franchising agreements in Australia, Ireland, New Zealand, and the United Kingdom. In April 2006 the company signed additional agreements in Spain and Taiwan. The franchise in the UK has grown to more than 100 sites around the country.

China?

We've been hesitant about China, but the need is clearly there. They have the one-child policy, so that child is looking at caring at some point for his or her parents and grandparents. I recently went there to talk with a prospective partner. The country's regions are very different— inland versus coast. We'll probably divide into provinces, realizing there are more children in the rural areas. In the cities there are huge high-rises, whereas the countryside is more spread out. The high-rises give us more options and certain economies of scale. For example, we could establish a function room in a high-rise where the seniors could socialize and reduce the sense of isolation. So things are moving forward there, but we've already started in Finland, Italy, and Singapore.

How does your business model deal with cultural differences?

There is something about U.S. culture that produces strong brands, among them many global franchising businesses. Senior care has been around forever. Our difference is that we do research, and work hard, to be a thought leader in the field and in the industry. We've built a premium brand. As such, we're sensitive to cultural differences, especially regarding food and food preparation. In Japan, we'd make miso soup for the client; in the U.S. it might be something different. There will also be differences in communicating: listening and speaking and the relationship in general. We provide training that's culturally relevant. Key is standardization, but flexible enough to accommodate cultural differences and preferences.

So the cultural dimension differentiates you to some extent; but can't anyone with compassion deliver these services in other countries?

In theory—yes. That's why we've worked hard to be judged a thought leader in the field of senior care. We conduct and sponsor research. We take this research and share it with people in the communities we serve. We apply other kinds of knowledge, including what's being learned about Alzheimer's and the people suffering from it. We turn this knowledge into training for the people who deliver the services. The challenge is to inform government and policy people of what we are doing and learning. Paul Hogan has been a member of the World Economic Forum for several years and goes to Davos, Switzerland, for the annual meeting. He's now vice-chair of a group looking at care for the elderly; the other main groups are energy and finance issues. It's significant that elder care is a top priority.

How do you find master franchisees and enter a new country?

We spend a long time finding the right partners who share our philosophy about caring for the elderly. The selection of good partners, training, and the building of relationships are the same key steps in the expansion of any franchise company internationally. We organize seminars in the country and invite local specialists, including elder law and elder care. A lot of what we do is to educate people and provide options. In terms of marketing, we do PR and provide testimonials. The master franchisees recruit the franchisees. For mature markets, the best source of clients is through hospitals and doctors. Hospitals, by far, provide the most referrals. The Web is very important for reaching the adult children. We pay to be in the top 10 listings of the important search engines.

> *"...it's not just about money, but about making a difference for the elderly with compassion and tender hearts."*

What has been your experience with U.S. or other government export assistance?

For one, the Commerce Department people help us find prospective partners. They identify potential partners whose profiles parallel the company's ideal qualifications, and prearrange meetings for us. They also help identify key players in senior care policy. I've worked with them for years, and they helped me in Poland. When I got to the U.S. I contacted the U.S. Commercial Service office in Omaha, Nebraska, where I received market research as well as export counseling, and requested partner searches that put me on the right path to entering the Japanese market. I went on a franchising trade mission to Japan, where our services were showcased at Japan's largest franchise show. That's where we met our Japanese partners. They are an excellent resource for learning about a country's cultural issues and regulations. We are now able to anticipate the challenges of new markets. We can depend on the U.S. Commercial Service to help us with overcoming licensing issues, finding the right partners, and additional challenges we may face in future endeavors. We use them to enter all overseas markets.

What's the biggest lesson learned in your work?

Caring for the elderly is one of the biggest social challenges of our time. Our concept is very meaningful, and it's not just about money, but about making a difference for the elderly with compassion and tender hearts. Doing business internationally presents many challenges, and for us it's finding people with the same core values and culture. We are fulfilling our mission of providing meaningful care for independent elders worldwide. Knowing the quality of life is being enhanced worldwide by our services makes me go to bed feeling good at night. ⬦

Melanie Bergeron
Chair of the Board,
Two Men and a Truck/International, Inc.

How did you get started in the moving business?

We never imagined being in the moving business—that is, until my mom and my brothers Brig and Jon scraped together some money to buy a truck to help raise extra cash for college. Although my brothers soon left the nest to attend school, mom knew a good idea when she saw one. In 1985, with $350, she started a company called Two Men and a Truck. We wouldn't have to worry about moving again and, more important, neither would our customers.

Believe it or not, moving is ranked as the third most stressful event, after death and divorce, so there is a real demand for a service that makes the customer king because he or she may be pretty sad and fearful. We don't want to add to their woes. Our goal is to do things right the first time. The most important concern customers have about moving is that the moving company be there when it says it will. So from Lansing, Michigan, we expanded our franchising concept across the U.S., with Mom serving as its founder and chief operating officer. In 2001 I was running day-to-day operations as president and chief operating officer. Brig is CEO and Jon is executive vice president. We had gross sales of $220 million in 2011 and that increased by $40 million in 2012. The franchises own 1,400 moving trucks and employ more than 5,600 workers, not counting support staff. The average franchise grosses $1,300,000 per year and will increase to $1,500,000 this year. We have 76 employees at headquarters.

That's a lot of moving and a lot more money than the $350 your mom started out with.

Yes. Americans move a lot, and that was still true during the recession and probably now. There are a lot of divorces and people have downsized and moved to rentals. Many elderly people also move, some to be nearer to their children as they age; others move from their homes to a retirement community. We market to seniors with large-type brochures and have a separate brochure for their children, focusing on the anxieties caused by moving, and how we as a company, and they as family members, can reduce those anxieties. Ultimately, we are not a moving company, but a service that helps people through excellent customer service. That's the key to the whole thing.

How does the concept work in other countries?

We are now in Canada, Ireland, and the UK. Gross revenues from international are 4 percent of total sales, but that's up from nothing. We have plans to expand to mainly English-speaking countries, including Australia and New Zealand. We are looking at Singapore. After that, China. We looked at Mexico but what we learned is that many Mexicans don't like the concept of two guys arriving at their house with a truck. It's a matter of trust and it doesn't seem to be there yet, at least not without a lot of branding work. In many countries there is a tradition of very low paid people doing this work. So it will take some education of the market and a better understanding of the opportunities than we currently have.

> "They want the U.S. brand power and mystique."

Have you thought of Dos Hombres or Two Blokes and a Lorry for your international franchises?

No, we need to stick to the brand because that's what the master franchisers and their investors want. They want the U.S. brand power and mystique. The customers are less interested in whether it's a U.S. brand. In fact, the appeal is the opposite. It's a local company that will be available when I need them.

What are the factors you look at when evaluating international opportunities?

The first is the size of the middle class, their mobility. These days there are powerful software tools that help us pinpoint income levels by neighborhood and whether the housing stock is single- or multi-family. Best areas for us are where there is a good mix. The pricing model will be different. We look at the regulations, such as are there restrictions on trucks carrying goods from city to city? What are the license and permit requirements? Are their obvious perceptions of acceptance of the service—good or bad? What is the competition and their pricing like, including other franchise moving companies? And when evaluating us, potential franchisees are asking whether we are making money for our franchisees. They want to know whether we are a fad. They want to know what the market will be like in 10 years for this service. They want to know how you can help block competition by providing superior IT, customer service, marketing, and training support. If you need help from local banks to get started, having a successful concept and track record behind you will help convince the finance people that you are a good risk. Venture capital likes us because we're mature with a lower risk profile. Many of our franchisees have equity partners.

How did you go global?

One of the biggest challenges was that our master franchisees were only just breaking into the export market. Fortunately, we had attended an International Franchise Association training seminar in Minneapolis, where we connected with Bill Edwards, president of Edwards Global Services, a consultancy company specializing in international franchising expansion. He told us that the biggest challenges for franchisers in going global is getting accurate market research and identifying potential master franchisees. In the case of Two Men and a Truck, we faced a third challenge known as market differentiation—otherwise, with plenty of moving businesses out there, why should a potential master franchisee in another country sign on with Two Men and a Truck? What makes it a cut above the rest?

We already had an answer to that question, and it's that we place an exceptional focus on customer service and sophisticated Web-based tracking systems. Those systems would enable potential master franchisees to monitor quality control and to improve performance measures such as labor costs and the time it takes to complete a move. The company's tracking systems created a potentially larger profit margin as compared with other moving companies. What Two Men and a Truck needed now was solid market research and a list of highly qualified prospects to convey their business model to potential master franchisees.

> "Don't cast a wide net when looking for potential partners. Instead, use the U.S. Commercial Service to target the best prospects."

Edwards Global Services was a long-term client of the U.S. Commercial Service in Newport Beach, and had used the office's export counseling and other services to help several premier franchise brands enter international markets. Among these programs was the Gold Key Service, which arranges business appointments abroad with potential foreign partners, all set up and prescreened by the U.S. Commercial Service. By 2003, Two Men and a Truck, through Edwards Global Services, worked with the U.S. Commercial Service to search for a franchise partner in Ireland. The company was assisted by the U.S. Commercial Service post in Ireland, whose commercial specialists provided key market research and designed a customized search strategy that included reaching out to databases of existing and potential master licensees. An advertisement was also placed in a local business newspaper highlighting the company's search for a master licensee. Then, in December 2003, Edwards met with nine qualified prospects in Dublin. Partially as a result of those meetings and ongoing follow-up by the U.S. Commercial Service and Edwards Global Services, Two Men and a Truck signed a master license for Ireland in May 2006 with DMG Services. The agreement was valued in excess of $300,000, and it included the rights for the UK market.

From a practical standpoint, going international protects our brand globally and lends credibility to the domestic market. Exporting also makes us more competitive and allows us to diversify our portfolio and weather changes in the economy. Ireland has had its problems, and the UK economy is weak. But Canada is booming and people are moving like crazy. Having a diverse portfolio helps us navigate the inevitable ups and downs and, of course, international is the way to grow. On the down side, return on investment on international takes time to grow. Flying support people around the world is a cost, but luckily there's a lot you can do online, including staff training.

What are the best marketing channels overseas?

The same as they are in the U.S. and Canada: search engine maximization with office location by postal code, and word of mouth.

What's your advice to folks contemplating starting or expanding their export business?

Don't cast a wide net when looking for potential partners. Instead, use the U.S. Commercial Service to target the best prospects. Being able to meet with reputable, motivated prospects really helped us in targeting our search efforts. Not only was it cost effective for us, but it would have taken months longer on our own to narrow down the best prospects. The U.S. Commercial Service is a source of information, market research, and due diligence that we know we can depend on when doing business around the world.

"Our goal is to do things right the first time.

We hired a consultant with international franchise experience to help us enter new markets. He's helping us now with Italy and Brazil. Other companies might want this expertise in house. And the consultant works with our federal government. This frees me up to do other things, including helping mentor new franchise concepts, including natural healing centers and places where you can work with paints while having a glass of wine. Another important thing is to register your trademark. Not enough people do this, and if you don't, it can really cost you a lot of money in the long run. Invest in good market research and personnel training to increase your chances for international franchising success, as buyers are becoming very sophisticated. Know the culture where you are going to do business. For example, when it comes to moving there are differences. Americans have so much stuff and bigger houses, while people in emerging markets have much less. In emerging markets, many families live together, but we are seeing a growing trend in the use of moving services as people don't wish to trouble their relatives by asking for their help when moving.

If you are a family business, don't be shy about moving the original hires out of key positions as business grows. Our domestic and international expansion required new expertise in IT, finance, and marketing. Once this expertise was in place, growth skyrocketed. Yes, franchising is a great industry, and it's creating a lot of jobs here in the U.S. and abroad. It's a great way to help people, and has brought us a lot of pleasure and satisfaction. ⬦

Sharon Doherty
Owner and Founder, Vellus Products

As the brains behind your pet cosmetics company, you have the perfect antidote for a bad fur day.

Yes, we do. The idea with Vellus is to glamorize with skin-safe products. We started back in 1993, and our formulas have never changed—for show dogs, which is our target market, and also pampered pets. We want those pets to be pampered, too. So you're right. We don't want anybody to have a bad fur day in the canine world and in the cat world.

And in the human world?

We don't advertise that, but I will tell you that the family does use this on ourselves because we know that there's nothing in there that would harm us. And they're quality products; they're high-end formulas. Shampoos for people don't work well on pets because animal skin is more sensitive than human skin and is more easily irritated. Most available pet shampoos, though sensitive to the skin, tend to leave hair unmanageable and without the glamour needed for the show dog or pampered pet.

You're in Columbus, Ohio, which has been hard hit in these tough economic times, but you've created this manufacturing company. And you fearlessly launched sales in a number of countries. Can you tell us about how that got started and where it's gone?

It started back in 1993. A Taiwan businessman had heard about us through the dog show network. He, being in Taipei, contacted me and wanted to buy some products in the amount of $25,000. And I had never exported before. Our company was new. The Taiwan buyer sold the product at some dog shows and I started getting calls from different countries. We quickly had to become knowledgeable with the help of the U.S. Commerce Department. John McCaslin, who was in the Cincinnati office back in that day, helped us a great deal to understand the process. And that was the beginning of it. If you have a good product in this market that we're in—the dog show network—word travels fast. And that was our first export, back in '93.

The reasons for not going global include that it's too risky, we're too small—only big companies export. It's just too complicated for us and we have a nice market here in the U.S., so why bother? How come that rationale didn't affect you way back in 1993?

I really believe that doing business overseas is a model of building relationships. And if you have a good product, it'll sell here, too, as well as overseas. There are a lot of good products on the market, but they don't go overseas because the people making them are a little bit afraid.

We never have done letters of credit. I know people feel the risk of not getting their money. From the outset, everything that leaves here is prepaid. Then we ship it out. And we've never had a problem. We'll soon be going into our 20th year. I think it is a wonderful venue because you meet so many cultures, but in this economy it is not the time to do cold business—everything has to be a warm business.

What do you mean by "warm"?

Cold business—my way of saying it is in the economy today and the way it's been for awhile, especially with big companies—they have a certain job description of doing this and then the other one has the job description of doing that. And that's OK because that's the way they have to run their large corporations. And we're a smaller manufacturing company and I'm, you might say, the "it" person. So I am the one who contacts potential overseas buyers. I check them out with the Commerce Department. And I can offer a warmer feeling. It's not such a cold business. It's more of a warmer-feeling business where they feel they have a friend. They have a support system and it's this person. And this is her name. And I can get in touch with her at any time because she's given me all her phone numbers.

I mean, small business is small business. And obviously, you would know the big conglomerates—Procter & Gamble and all those—they're big business. And that's wonderful. We need that. I mean, we need the big businesses. But the small businesses are losing out if they think they can't export too because it takes a certain kind of product. If you have a product and it works, there is a venue for you in the international marketplace.

I think our model has proved to be successful. And that is getting to know the people, letting them know that if they register their business with us to buy our products, we will help them make it happen. That's after checking them out and knowing they're serious, we will make it happen. They have to be agreeable to a minimum order, which is a certain amount of money—a certain amount of product. And then after that, there is no minimum.

We provide a strong support system, including designated people to talk to. It's either me or my daughter, Terry. We both do this. I'm the one who makes all the decisions, but still she understands how to fill their orders and they can talk to her, too. The main thing is, warm business is having someone that they can contact that they know is going to help them, that's going to back them up. When we find an overseas buyer, I welcome them into the family, the Vellus family. So it's a small business that thinks big.

Some commentators say that when it comes to the role that small businesses play in the overall international economy, they are not achieving what they are capable of. How many countries are you selling to?

We're in 34 countries selling to businesses in each of them. And we're talking now with Ecuador, Brazil, and the Dominican Republic. Brazil we have a contract with. The other two we've just started communicating with. They just sent information to me—communicated to me that they would like to sell our products in their country. We do not have a distributor in Ecuador and the Dominican Republic, so I'm very interested. And we take our time doing this. They don't feel any pressure. I have to know that they really want to do this. But 34 countries—I am thrilled about this. I feel very humble that we were able to accomplish this. And especially selling in Russia, Poland, Hungary, China, the Czech Republic. We have them sign an agreement that we've used since 1993. It's an "at will" agreement and can end if they leave the dog show business or we decide they are not performing up to expectations.

Latvia?

Latvia. Yeah, Lithuania. The Baltic states. Yeah, we're in Thailand, South Korea—you know, 34 countries. And they're listed on our website at vellus.com. You know, clicking on international distributors on the sidebar of our page, it tells all the countries we're in and soon, hopefully, we'll be adding Brazil, the Dominican Republic, and Ecuador. And we are also still speaking to Israel. I'm very interested in the products getting into Israel and, actually, they do show dogs there.

Do all these countries represent a single sale: "Chalk up Ecuador and then rush off to the next country," or are you actually doing repeat sales in most of those country markets?

Absolutely, it's repeat sales. First of all, from us to the end user, if I sell to them one time and I don't hear from them, then we do not have a good product and what we're saying doesn't work. And that's not the case. The product is good, the product line—the five basic grooming formulas are water based, safe for hair and skin. We've already done our homework here—took 2 years and did our homework. So my feeling is, once they try it we've got them. I always tell groomers and I always tell handlers, you know what you're doing in your country. You know how to groom the dog, but I know these formulas. And allow me to help you get the best from the formulas because these formulas can make your dogs look better than any other product that's on the market.

As far as the distributors are concerned, a distributor that orders once and I don't hear from them, they hear from me. Not in a bad way—in a warm way. "Is there anything we can do for you? We want to touch base and we're thinking about putting an ad in your local paper and would like to include maybe one of your customers' champions or something like that in an ad." We're actually doing that in *Top Notch Toys* magazine in a future issue. We're putting Latvia's Maltese in a full-page color ad. And so we've become friends with these people. You know, just like Mr. Bang in South Korea, a wonderful person—has never been here. We've never met in person. We've only become friends through the email. However, he's been with us for years. We got a big, big letter the other day from somebody in business that wanted to take over what he's doing. But we're very loyal to the people who sell for us. And so I copied his information to these people and I also copied him on the email. He wrote back and he's always been very professional, very businesslike, a man of few words. And I respect that. But he wrote back and he was so thrilled. He said, in his words, "I always do business with you. I will always do business with you. Thank you, thank you for what you've done." In other words, we gave him the business. We didn't take the business. We gave it to him because we'll make business through him and because it's the right thing to do,

So it is a support system, being a support system to these people that you've built a relationship with. And they know you won't hurt them. You have to help the people that are selling for you. It's very personal for me. I love people. I mean, for me, it's easy because I enjoy doing what I do. I'm 73 years old. I enjoy coming to work every day.

Two days ago in the evening—I have an office in my home for international—I called China and I talked to Joey Lee and I said, "We have your order. It'll soon be ready. And I'll send you the invoice and you can wire the money." She said, "Oh, I'm so glad." And I talk to her probably three times a year. So it isn't like we talk all the time—and I don't pressure them. But they know that I have a reputation in this world, in this market that I'm in, that I will help people and not hurt people. But we do have to make money. And we do have to—everybody has to make money. We do and I want them to. And I will help them make money.

There was one country where nothing was happening with orders, so I called them. I tend to if I think there's a problem. Rather than email or send a letter, I tend to just pick up the phone. And I called them and there was sickness in the family and they were having problems. I said, "Well, let me know if there's anything we can do from here. And if you need inventory, let me know and we'll get it to you quickly. You don't have to buy a lot. Just buy what you need to get you through." So you have to give and take.

Was that call to a distributor in China? Might there have been a cultural factor in the nonresponse?

Yes, it's possible. The call and other communication may have put this person on the spot. It could have embarrassed him, caused him to lose face. What I thought was warm may not have been received that way. You have to be ready to modify your approach when dealing with different cultures.

What have you learned about cultural differences?

Vellus shampoos and other products can easily be varied for different grooming techniques. In England, dog exhibitors prefer less poofy topknots than those on show dogs in the U.S., where owners tend to be more exotic with topknots. There also can be different preferences for the look of show dogs.

What advice do you have for people contemplating starting or expanding their exports?

I was once duped by a businessman from another country who said he knew all about the pet market there. I followed some of his advice, and it caused me to lose customers in that country. Always do a thorough check on your potential business partners. Gather as much information as you can. Don't make any assumptions; the wrong choice can cost your business valuable time and money. Our embassies can do these checks, and you can search online or call the U.S. Commercial Service.

Exporting has changed my life. I love exporting because it has enabled me to meet so many people from other cultures. Exporting has made me more broad minded, and I have developed a great appreciation for other cultures and the way others live their lives. You are put in contact with real people on the other side.

You have a couple of parrots there. They don't use the shampoo, do they?

No, they get sprayed with water every other day. They sing. Oh my goodness, they sing. We have one bird that sings, "Oh, what a beautiful morning. Oh, what a beautiful day." And then he goes into "Jesus Loves Me"—the whole song of "Jesus Loves Me"—goes right into it! ∅

Kusum & Mukund Kavia
Owners, Combustion Associates, Inc.

What do the Combustion Associates do? Combust?

Well, you're very close. We do power generation systems, using aeroderivative turbines. And that would be your aircraft or military turbines. Our company provides modular power plants in the range from 1-megawatt to 10-megawatt. A 1-megawatt is the size of a 40-foot container and can power 1,000 U.S. homes. We've focused on a smaller piece of the pie. So, when we take it to emerging countries such as [in] Africa, which is a growing market right now, or Eastern Europe or Central America, they can power villages. When a customer buys a number of our smaller units instead of one big one from a competitor, if one goes down for maintenance there are others to take up the slack. If a bigger 20-megawatt plant goes down, you're in trouble. Our units also operate on and off the power grid, can be powered with alternative fuels, and can be moved around.

We started our business in 1991 when we were a two-person office in a 200-square-foot facility. Today, we have grown to 60 employees with a 40,000-square-foot facility, and 90 percent of our revenues come from exporting. We are into about 10 countries. The product that we are in is not the number of countries; it's the dollar amount. The dollar amount is pretty substantial for us. And we are into Africa, which is a growing market right now, and Central America and Asia. Those are our three major markets, and Eastern Europe.

Are you both engineers by training?

I am an engineer and my wife trained in business management. We were both born in Kenya, where our parents immigrated from India. We came to the U.S. via England and Canada.

What was the biggest challenge you faced in getting started in the international marketplace?

The biggest challenge we faced is that we weren't a brand name. We were not recognized in the industry. So, being a small company, we had to make a name for ourselves out there. We've done that in a number of ways, including our website, going to trade shows, getting referrals from bigger companies in the power generation industry, and working with U.S. government agencies.

How do the bigger companies help you? Aren't they competitors?

There are not many competitors now. In the U.S., the big power generation companies like GE are not so interested in our part of the market, the 1- to 10-megawatt. Also, we use some of their equipment in building our plants. So for these and other reasons, when GE is traveling around the world, if they encounter a need for smaller plants, they'll sometimes refer us. As we've gotten more experience, GE, for example, has asked us to speak on doing business in Africa at some of their events. This helps with networking within the industry and leads to more contacts and referrals. There is growing competition in our market segment, especially from China, but also Japan and India.

Mukund Kavia (right) meets a customer in Ghana.

What help did you get from the government organizations in the U.S.?

We used partnerships with the U.S. government, including the U.S. Commercial Service, that spread our name, that spread what we did, and that really elevated us to a level that we were able to then be in front of the customer at the international level. The local U.S. Commercial Service office in Ontario, California, helped us by doing a lot of background research on best markets. They showed us the right way to do it. And when we brought the potential customers to the U.S., they accommodated them in every sense possible. One of the biggest things that I remember is the U.S. Commercial Service director opening his office to us. At that time we had a small business and didn't have a room to accommodate this delegation that was coming. We actually had our customers meet us at the U.S. Commercial Service office in Ontario and utilize their conference room. The representative of the Export-Import Bank of the United States was invited to talk about loan programs for foreign buyers to purchase U.S. equipment and services. So we had all these resources together under one roof, and our customers were very impressed. Now the U.S. Commercial Service brings potential buyers to us who are visiting the U.S.

The U.S. Commercial Service also publishes Energy Alerts, which are emails from Commerce Department foreign service officers stationed around the world. The emails summarize information and business opportunities in the energy sector. They also include information on Requests For Proposals and Requests For Quotations that we can respond to. We've definitely gotten some business from these efforts.

Do you often invite customers and prospects to the U.S.?

Yes. In about 60 percent of the cases they come here, and we go to them in 40 percent of the cases. These are high-value purchases, and each installation is different. If they come here, we know they are serious. You really do need to sit down and talk together. They need to see where we do the construction and how we did it. Meet our team members. It really helps improve communication and relationships.

> "...customers appreciate dealing with the owners of the company..."

> "...willingness to go places and to build relationships with people and to deliver excellent customer service [are] important..."

You exhibit a kind of fearlessness in jumping on airplanes to do business in some unusual places.

Fearless maybe, but not reckless. We do our due diligence, often asking our embassies overseas to do background checks on potential customers. Mukund is very comfortable doing business in other countries, whether it's sitting down with village elders, and it sometimes is, or whoever might be involved in the purchase decision or affected by the installation. We're both originally from Africa so this is probably part of it. There's also a big advantage to us jumping on planes and being accessible to the customer. I think a main reason why we're successful is that the customers appreciate dealing with the owners of the company they are buying hardware and services from. We are available to them and they can contact us directly with their questions and concerns. Reacting quickly is important, and nobody likes getting bounced around. Because we're small, our costs are lower, making us more affordable to customers in developing countries. Customers also like the fact we are from the U.S. and that U.S. brands are used in our power plants. I think the willingness to go places and to build relationships with people and to deliver excellent customer service are more important than being from a particular place. In this sense, many more Americans could be successful doing business in these parts of the world.

Have you learned things doing business abroad that have made you a better company?

You always come back with new knowledge. You see hardships. You see people struggling with things we take for granted. You want to help them to live better. If we can't help them, we try and connect them with others in our network who can. You learn to listen attentively and to show respect. You definitely learn how to find solutions that were not automatically in your toolbox. One of the biggest things we learned is about the installation and maintenance process, which is different in every place we go. By listening and carefully observing how people do things, we have made changes in our designs, the fabrication of our components, and in our training of local people that have helped us in all the markets we sell to.

What new markets are you looking at?

We are negotiating with some Iraqi customers, who very much need our products. We have a contract for plants providing 240 megawatts in Bangladesh. And we expect to have projects in the Philippines and, surprisingly, in Italy.

What advice would you give companies that are starting out and have not yet thought about going to another country to sell their products and services?

Don't limit yourself. You're already doing something that you know, that is your passion. All you have to do is, yes, get out of your comfort zone. You're going to have different challenges—some new, some old. But I would encourage everyone who is looking to export to say please, "Why haven't you thought of

"We used partnerships with the U.S. government, including the U.S. Commercial Service, that spread our name, that spread what we did, and that really elevated us to a level that we were able to then be in front of the customer at the international level.

doing that?" The government, both at the local, state, and federal level, really go out of their way to help businesses blossom and grow. And we have found that everywhere we have gone and told people about our story, they have opened up and said, "How can we help you?" So this is a wonderful dream that we're living, and we hope to do even better in the future.

We're a family-owned business and we really have the American story, since both Mukund and I were immigrants. We came to this country with very little, but lots of big dreams. And so, America to us still remains the land of opportunity. We just worked hard, and failure was not an option for us. So every day, in and out, our business is our passion. As Americans, I believe that all of us want to reinvent ourselves. And this is true for both Mukund and I. We are immigrants; we want to reinvent ourselves, and we want to be the best we can be so that we are able to export U.S. products overseas that are quality, cost effective and really a win-win for the countries that we're doing business with. ∅

Jimmy Wu
Founder and CEO, Infinity Air

How did your business get started?

I was born in Shanghai, China, and immigrated to the U.S. with my parents when I was 9 years old. In 1979 I became a U.S. citizen. I've always had a passion for business and aviation. I started as a grunt—filing and copying for an aviation company in Van Nuys, California. I worked my way up and eventually got the Avianca Airlines account. I introduced a concept that at the time was new in the industry. The concept involved managing the entire parts procurement process for the airline. Instead of per-piece purchasing, the concept was a strategic relationship with the customer for a flat fee. We managed consumption, source material, and use of the parts. We used the company's purchasing power to get better prices. It was a one-year agreement and at the end of that year we had saved the customer 28 percent on their parts bill. They signed up for 8 more years.

That got the boss's attention and made me believe that I could apply outside-the-box thinking in other places. So I started my own company in 1977, based on this concept. Affinity Air is a manufacturer and distributor of new and refurbished aircraft parts for the commercial aerospace industry. We serve thousands of customers around the world each year. Most of the time the customer sends us the aircraft part and we send them a new one. We'll then repair the old one and put it in our inventory. Occasionally, technical experts from our team will work on site in the foreign country on projects such as scanning the aircraft for structural integrity or major installations. We sold $63 million in products and services to customers in 60 countries, with the export of aircraft parts alone accounting for more than half of our total worldwide sales.

Five aircraft manufacturers account for 80 percent of Infinity Air's repairs and spare parts, including Boeing. We service mainly Boeing's 737-600-900 series, 767

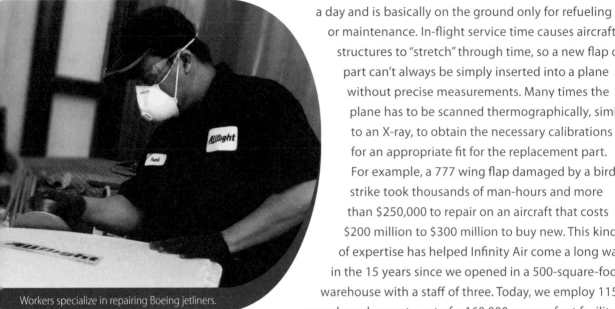
Workers specialize in repairing Boeing jetliners.

twin-aisle, 747-400, and 777 aircraft. People are often surprised when I tell them that the 777 averages 18 hours of flight time a day and is basically on the ground only for refueling or maintenance. In-flight service time causes aircraft structures to "stretch" through time, so a new flap or part can't always be simply inserted into a plane without precise measurements. Many times the plane has to be scanned thermographically, similar to an X-ray, to obtain the necessary calibrations for an appropriate fit for the replacement part. For example, a 777 wing flap damaged by a bird strike took thousands of man-hours and more than $250,000 to repair on an aircraft that costs $200 million to $300 million to buy new. This kind of expertise has helped Infinity Air come a long way in the 15 years since we opened in a 500-square-foot warehouse with a staff of three. Today, we employ 115 people and operate out of a 160,000-square-foot facility, with two additional locations: Seattle and Miami.

We opened the Miami office in 2003. We did it for our Latin America customers, specifically for TAM, the Brazilian airline. That same year we opened the Kent, Washington, facility. It was an old FAA repair station specializing in cockpit windows. We rebuilt it and enlarged it to repair flight service controls.

What got you into international?

This business is global. Airplanes fly from one country to another. Many countries have airlines; some have many. Infinity Air launched exports in our first year, entering the Chinese and Korean markets. I'm impressed with the opportunities in Korea, and it has become our largest export destination. Last year, sales of everything from flight-service controls and engines to interior equipment and cockpit windows totaled more than $10 million. While Korea has always been a good market for Infinity Air, it's getting even better now with the U.S.–Korea Free-Trade Agreement. It put a spring in the step of our business there. Korea is a huge market for us, and with the trade agreement in place, the market just got a whole lot bigger. We've already seen a spike in sales, with new orders coming from the Korean government for maintenance on regional jets, helicopters, and other aircraft—and I wouldn't be surprised to see a 20 percent growth in our sales this year alone as a direct result of the agreement. Prior to the trade agreement, servicing Korea's aviation market required payment of Korean tariffs of up to 15 percent on spare parts. For example, if an airline customer in Korea shipped an engine to Infinity Air's facilities in Los Angeles, Seattle, or Miami for a repair requiring $50,000 in spare parts, the customer would have to pay hundreds or thousands of additional dollars just to cover the tariffs alone. Now, the tariffs have either been removed or are in the process of being phased out, giving Infinity Air more leverage for competitive pricing.

Do you need that leverage, especially with your competitors in Asia?

When a company like ours is competing with businesses in China, Russia, and Europe for international sales, the more tools we have to stay competitive, the better—and that's where the free-trade agreement is so critical. We've found it also gives the Koreans more access to our market and makes it easier for financing. The trade agreement also makes things more predictable for lenders, and we've had a much easier time getting loans from local banks here in California. Even with this leverage, my company can't compete on a dollar-per-hour basis with China and other Asian countries. We can compete on innovation and business process. Because of these processes, we perform the service in less time and have a strong reputation for reliability and technical support—that's the key to our international success.

How do you do that?

I mentioned one example—rethinking this business in terms of being partners with customers and managing their parts procurement and repair. We constantly try to be imaginative in everything we do—to make the best products, deliver the best service. My parents came here when I was 9. They wanted a better life. In China, they looked at Coca-Cola like it was a dream. The advertising, the shape of the bottle, the taste itself. They said, "We don't have things like this." There were no high standards involved in the products that were made in China at the time. I looked at aviation through my parents' eyes: build a product that people in an industry need.

So China can compete on price, but not as well on ideas?

Yes. The Chinese don't have the imagination piece. This may be a cultural thing that's very hard to change. We have that in this country. Some countries are good at copying things. They are content takers, not makers. As a result, the takers are hiring Americans to do the imagination part because we are content makers. Just look at Apple. No surprise that most Asian car manufacturers design the cars here. Freedom is an integral part of this, and the Chinese don't have it and probably won't for the foreseeable future.

Part of imagination is sustainability. We consider that in everything we do. Sustainability is key. I insist that we use printer paper on both sides. Some of my employees say "This is so mom-and-pop business." I say, "No, this is about money we throw away." Sustainability generates imagination when you are forced to look at the whole process, the whole life cycle, as we do with everything we repair and sell. We work not with just the immediate customer but with the people who recycle the metal parts at the end of the parts' life. Some of this is cultural, too. In the Chinese culture, at meals we eat together and the food is shared. Everyone takes only what they need. In the West, everyone has their own plate, often heaped with more than they need.

How do you introduce your employees to the importance of imagination and innovation?

It's not easy and takes time. We start by telling people that they are unconscious and unskilled, and that at the end of the process they will be conscious and skilled. And finally they will be unconscious and skilled. In other words, looking at things in new ways will become second nature; they won't have to think about doing that.

That sounds very Southern California.

We're all doing it, including me. We think it works. When we say you are unconscious and unskilled, don't take it personally; it's not a criticism. The goal is unconscious and skilled. The goal is for insights to become second nature. It's a long process.

Can't imagining and reimagining be used for bad ends?

Yes. It can be used to imagine new ways to cook the books, to increase stock value by false and fraudulent practices. Now there is more emphasis on using imagination to increase paper profits, and we have in many cases forgotten how to make things well. The bad uses of imagination are the reason I chose to start my own company because of the practices of a previous employer.

A technician repairs a wing.

What's your experience been with government programs to help exporters?

We've benefited from the trade expertise of the U.S. Commercial Service. In 2010, for example, Infinity Air was looking to expand long-term partnership opportunities in Korea and sought counseling from the U.S. Commercial Service staff in Los Angeles and the U.S. Embassy in Korea. Soon after, I was encouraged to sign up for the U.S. Commercial Service Aerospace Executive Service, a business matchmaking program that took place at the 2010 Singapore Air Show. We were looking to build long-term, strategic partnerships with major airlines in Korea, and at the show, we were introduced to different airline representatives in meetings arranged by the U.S. Commercial Service. It turned out to be a good move, as we ended up signing a representative agreement with an airline that has greatly expanded our presence in Korea. There's no question it would have been much more difficult and time-consuming for us if we had tried to make this connection on our own. We also got firsthand insights into the legal and financial aspects of doing business in Korea that were key to making the deal happen. With continued government help we're now making sales to aerospace operators in Turkey, Japan, Vietnam, Singapore, Indonesia, India, and Panama. Exporting has enabled us to buffer the ups and downs of a tough economy, and made us a better company by forcing us to face the reality of global competition. Since 2008 we've doubled our export sales, which shows what can be achieved with a good product and superior customer service.

The other thing the government does for us is regulation. The FAA sets very high safety and quality standards for every part we sell. When we put the FAA-approved label on the parts we sell and work we do, it's really the gold standard in the industry. No other country has this kind of credibility. It's message is "Don't worry. We've got you covered." FAA inspectors are here and in our hair nearly every day. We're glad to see them.

You seem bullish on the future.

I am. It has been more than 30 years since my parents overcame hardships in China to bring our family to the U.S. Looking back, I'm so happy to have realized the dream of becoming an American and running an internationally successful business. In fact, I'm living the American Dream every day—and enjoying every second. ⌀

Pierce Barker
Cofounder, ProStuff LLC

How did you get started?

ProStuff LLC was founded in 2004 by me and a couple of friends. The business idea was our inspiration meeting the opportunity. A customer came walking through the door one day and needed help with a piece of equipment that he had built, and from that, we saw the opportunity to take this product—a starting gate for bicycle racing—on an international basis. I had some expertise in hydraulics, skills learned from my dad. The starting gate is a pretty sophisticated piece of gear. Add pumps to fabricated sheet metal and some other devices—and the race is on.

The gate is especially popular with BMX—bicycle motocross. BMX employs a small course of about 400 meters that includes jumps and tabletops. I'm going to guess that there are somewhere around 500,000 riders, just pure riders, in the entire world, at various levels. And they are in every country, in developing countries, throughout the world. And our biggest customer set is not just the consumer, but the actual sports teams. When you look at the people that are involved in the sports team, coaching, and the international Olympic efforts throughout the world, there's got to be several million people involved with just the sport of BMX. And then add in the mountain biking and it's even bigger.

What was your biggest challenge starting out?

The market in the U.S. wasn't as big as I had thought. So the company had to go global—fast. The biggest challenge was to generate international sales quickly and to produce a high-quality product. As a startup manufacturing company with six employees we can't afford the cost of shipping equipment back and forth over great distances for repair. To be successful we needed from the get-go to take a durable, reliable product to the world. But customers were not individual bikers; they were organizations that sponsor the races. Where to find them, and if you did find them would they buy?

Then what happened?

I did some research and estimated that worldwide there are several million people involved with just the sport of BMX. If mountain biking is added, the market is much bigger. Contacting the riders was out of the question, so we decided to get ProStuff's starting gate adopted as the industry standard.

Pierce Barker (left) with a Colombia racer sponsored by ProStuff.

We found that BMX was going to be part of the 2008 Olympics, and I said, "The best way to advertise our products is to go to the very top of the sport and go to work with those guys—become the international specification and let that filter down." And that's exactly what we did. I picked up the phone and called the Union Cycliste Internationale in Switzerland. Of the person who answered, I asked: "Who do we talk to get our products specified and used in the Olympics?" The person in Switzerland answered: "That would be me." That call was how it started.

Brand building at the Olympics was huge, but insufficient to generate enough orders or to provide the financing needed to fill them. I had no idea what to do when we first started. We were plowing new ground every day. Then I talked to local government folks and learned about the Export-Import Bank of the U.S. ProStuff applied and was accepted into the Bank's loan guarantee program, which provides working capital to U.S. exporters at competitive rates. With the Bank's assistance and that of the U.S. Commerce Department you can't stop us. We can go anywhere. Since 2005 when ProStuff made its first export, the company has set up distribution on five continents, and sold products to customers in 41 countries—so far. And we're about to add a couple new ones today.

Do you have a written export plan? Most small companies don't.

One of the basic concepts that we looked at is to make it simple and easy and flexible to do what we really need. We built a one-page business plan and then went out and executed it. And it's not fraught with a lot of details and 27 pages of specifications. It says, go do this. We want to be the number one race-gate provider in the world in the sports of BMX and mountain biking.

And it's a success-oriented business plan. Probably the number one thing: starting off with understanding what you want to do and where you want to go. And the number two thing is incorporating the concept of velocity in your business. And when I say velocity, we're talking about instantaneous response to our customers' needs and requests. And I think that's really key. It's not uncommon for us to get a phone call from some customer in North America needing some equipment—a smaller customer—and we can turn that request into a shipped order in less than 12 hours in some cases. We like a week. But we can actually do it in 12 hours if they really need it.

And we've taken that whole philosophy to the world, to try to respond quickly. We do this with shipping and with everything we do. The third thing that I think is really important here is: We made a conscious business decision that we're going to produce the very best product in the world. Another way to say that is, we don't make junk. And through that, our business reputation over the last several years has grown from when we first started, being a pariah—nobody wanted to deal with us, look at us, talk to us—to the point where, now, on a daily basis, we have incoming requests for quotations from all over the world.

Your goal of being number one in the world sounds like a pretty tall order for a company of six employees in the middle of what's referred to as "the Rust Belt."

I have a sign that I walk by every day in my office. It's just a little badge that I picked up a few years ago. It says, "The difficult, we do immediately. The impossible takes a little longer. Miracles by appointment only." If we find something we can't do, we figure out how to do it. And we just go out there. There are places where you wouldn't think that this sport exists, things that are off the political radar for the U.S. because of situations with those countries.

> 'The market in the U.S. wasn't as big as I had thought. So the company had to go global—fast."

Specifically, two come to mind immediately: Bolivia and Zimbabwe. The political situations in those countries are really, really difficult. And we have established successful distribution in both countries. And where we couldn't get support through some of our programs because of the restrictions, the political restrictions, we said, "You know what? We're going to figure out how to make it work," and we've done it.

So one of the important aspects, and something to put on your plan, is challenge the conventional wisdom. Don't accept taken-for-granted assumptions, and rely on your gut and the personal relationship, even in a place like Zimbabwe, where most people would not want to go because of the news that they have read in the newspaper. I was in South Africa a few months ago, and I'll be back there again in a couple of months. They invited me to come up for a weekend, and I wasn't really sure I wanted to go. And they're fearless. Those people are absolutely fearless and champions of freedom, but it's a difficult political situation. Nobody, really, in the U.S. . . . the common person in the U.S. never has the opportunity to see that, and all we have is fear of those things.

Has language been a barrier for you?

I speak French, but most of the people that I deal with anywhere in the world are bi- or trilingual, and we have never found that the languages have been a barrier. We've just decided to work through it, and we've been successful at it. In the last 12 hours, I've been in contact with China. I looked at this morning, just real quickly: China, Latvia, Switzerland, Denmark, and Singapore. And we actually received a contract from China this morning, and it's our contract. It's not their contract. They signed ours.

You're in or on the fringes of the Rust Belt, which has been hit very hard with high unemployment. President Obama has challenged us to double exports within the next 5 years. Some people have scoffed already. What do you think of our chances, here, of pulling ourselves out of this and regaining some of our manufacturing prowess, helping the economy and generating some new jobs?

Manufacturing, back 15 years ago, accounted for—I think it was in the area of 36 percent of our gross domestic product. And today, it's down around 18, I think, the last time I checked. And the problem with that is that those are the real valuable jobs. It's where you take something—you take an idea and some raw materials, and you convert it into a product. We want to do that just in the U.S. But we have to go to other places in the world and take the technology that we've developed. We're really good at technology, but we haven't been good at purveying it. And, philosophically, we have to take that technology to the rest of the world. And that's been one of the core principles in our success. We've implemented the technology throughout the world, and the quality of our products has set us up for the next order. That's how that happens. It's kind of a relay race that we're doing.

The market for bicycle racing starting gates is global.

A few things have happened since we last talked. Can you update us?

I am still traveling a great deal. I just finished the Olympics in England—sold some more "stuff" there. I got back from Vancouver, B.C., Sunday night and sold some "stuff." We continue to purvey American products to all corners of the globe, with equipment in more than 40 countries now. Competition out of Europe is much stronger, and trying to take the market away from us. We're not letting that happen. We are negotiating for the Olympics in Rio in 2016 and hope to be successful with that. Still making money but being pressed hard by the downturn in the

> **"The company has set up distribution on five continents, and sold products to customers in 41 countries ... And we're about to add a couple new ones today."**

economy again. My business partner, Ed Doherty, died unexpectedly last year, August 19, 2011. It has been very difficult to make it through that but we are still here and we survived. The world has become a very transparent, flat place for us. We can get our parts delivered to New Zealand or England in 4 days or less. It's amazing, and we are embracing all the changes. I'm continuing to operate on the basis of some cherished principles. Keep your word to your customers; they are your best salesmen. Respect their culture and speak the language of your customers, be it Spanish or Chinese, even if it's just a few words. Treat everyone fairly. You don't have to be cheap. Never build junk. Underclaim your virtues and oversupport your product. Constantly improve your technology. Skate to where the puck is going to be. Build the best stuff. Never stop being the best in class, in competition, in business, and ultimately you will win. We just never stop trying to improve. ∅

Bobby Patton
Patton Electronics Company

What do you make and how did you get started?

It's an electronics manufacturing company that my younger brother and I started together in 1984 when we were still students at the University of Maryland. He was majoring in computer science and I was as well. He later changed to marketing, which was good for us because it enabled us to really start thinking about business. We began by selling small electronic widgets that would interface between dumb terminals and IBM mainframe computers; so that was a long time ago, before PCs were really popular. Our business has just migrated into newer and newer technologies over time. We have about a thousand products in our portfolio. Our biggest-selling products right now are in voice-over IP.

How did you got into the international side of things?

We were obviously in the technology business. So we were tracking what was going on with the Internet from very early days. Before there was a World Wide Web, there was the Internet, and we were playing around with email and those sorts of things throughout the 1980s. When the World Wide Web really started to take off, we were very early in getting a domain name and putting our corporate presence on the Web, and started to find international customers interested in our products. So after a few queries came in—mostly from Europe, mostly from English-speaking parts of the world—we decided to make a trip in the late 1980s, early 1990s, over to England and Western Europe and identify prospective channel partners that could sell our products in those markets.

How did you do that? You just don't get on a plane and fly into a city and start opening the phone book.

Actually, we did go into these various cities and opened the phone book and looked for companies that were in the communication space. We had some leads through the Internet, so we knew that there were some companies that we could visit. But once we got there we looked up other companies that were en route between our already scheduled visits and made additional stops along the way. Direct mail was a very popular thing in the U.S. So we began exploring direct mail marketing companies and identifying companies that would have the right profile to sell our products in those markets and reach out to them through regular email or postal mail correspondents.

It was a pretty brave thing to show up in a foreign city, where you had never been, with a phone book in hand. Were you a little bit, you know, anxious?

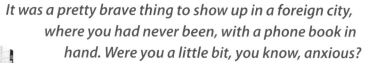

Patton is bullish on the future of U.S. manufacturing.

Not really. My father was a serial entrepreneur. He also had a history in electronics. He was one of Hewlett-Packard's first five sales guys, selling through a rep organization—independent sales rep. So he had a lot of experience. That business led him into used equipment. And he found that the biggest market for used American goods was actually overseas. And he established some really strong contacts in Israel.

So right when we were starting our business we went to Israel and met with some of his friends. They had products that they had designed in Israel. We added them to our product portfolio and started selling them in the U.S. So we had a little bit of international exposure through my father.

So your dad was an inspiring figure. Not only did he have these connections, but probably just in the way he talked to you and your brother growing up.

He modeled a lot of things for us. My father is a father of 10 children, so a big family. We used to gather around the dinner table, and he would have business meetings at the dinner table with a lot of us kids listening in. So it was just part of the culture growing up—conducting business at home and working with international reps and channels.

Do you have children now? And are passing that same interest in the world on to them?

Yeah. I have five children. My wife is very active with two foreign student exchange programs. One is AFS (American Field Service). She traveled to Norway when she was in high school. She also works with an organization called Amicus. They bring students from foreign countries over to the U.S. So we have foreign students living with us pretty regularly, and foreign visitors. And we've taken our children on international travel as well.

They'll be fully equipped to play their role, whatever it might be, in the greater world.

We hope that they get the idea that the world really is flat, that there's lots of opportunity around the globe. And they need to look outside our country.

Give us a little sense of the scope of your international business at this stage and how it's grown.

We have been growing pretty steadily. International was a very small part of our business when we started out. At this point, international revenue is about 75 percent of our business. We have active channels—thousands of active resale channels in about 125 different countries. So we've been to virtually every continent that has a city. Been there and set up channels and are selling our products into those markets. We have about a hundred employees in Maryland. And we have our manufacturing facility in Gaithersburg, which is also another rare thing. We manufacture our products here in the U.S.—electronics, nonetheless, and in voice-over IP—so we make Internet devices in the U.S. and ship them around the world.

We have about a hundred employees outside the U.S., mostly in sales and technical support roles. A big part of our go-to-market strategy is to be able to communicate with our customers in their language. So we have local language capability for technical support and for sales as well.

It sounds like a complicated operation.

We consider ourselves a micro-multinational. So we're fairly small, but we have all the complexities of a multinational company.

Would you say that your experience could serve as a model for other U.S. companies that would like to manufacture here and sell what they manufacture internationally?

Absolutely. I can just tell you from my experience that the U.S. has a brand recognition around the world as being a quality manufacturing location, and so U.S. products are very well received around the world. We have a leg up compared to most other countries that are manufacturing these days. We have a competitive advantage just because of our brand recognition. So there's huge opportunity there. The biggest thing that keeps people from entering new markets and new spaces is fear. And it's mostly fear of the unknown. What I can say is that people are people everywhere I go, that it's really enjoyable to get to know people in other markets. They have families and kids too; they are trying to make money and they have a lot of the same motivations. It's very easy to get along with people once you start talking the language of commerce.

So why is it that while some U.S. manufacturing capability is being hollowed out many are rather pessimistic about the future of U.S. manufacturing?

I think the future for U.S. manufacturing is bright. And I think that there's a big push to move manufacturing back to the U.S., re-sourcing from the local markets. It is true that the more outsourcing that you do, the more of the legacy knowledge you lose in the things that you used to make and the things that you used to manufacture. But the manufacturing world has changed, too. And there's a lot more automation going on, and a lot more of what used to be really skilled labor has been automated—and there's machinery. And so now the skills that we need are people who can effectively run machines. So while yes, we do lose some talent and some capability when we see manufacturing going overseas, there's also an opportunity to change the way we're doing manufacturing and to change the way that we think about manufacturing and change the way that we educate for manufacturing jobs. And I think that's where the U.S. has a great opportunity.

You say that working with government agencies in the U.S. has helped expand your export business. Not everybody's wild about working with government agencies these days.

We've worked pretty extensively with the Export-Import Bank of the U.S. As a matter of fact, that's been a key component for us in financing our foreign receivables. Domestic banks are going to be a little bit nervous about whether or not they'll be able to collect on receivables that are coming from Sri Lanka or some other country in the world that they're not familiar with. And so the Ex-Im Bank provides some stability for the commercial banks in lending to organizations like mine.

We've used the U.S. Department of Commerce on a number of occasions, particularly when we're trying to penetrate new markets. We just opened an office in Hungary, and I had a lot of interactions with the folks at the embassy in Hungary, as we are trying to really open up the market in Eastern Europe—in the Balkans—getting to know what's going on in Croatia and Bosnia and Serbia, and the opportunities there, and in other venues. It wasn't so long ago that we had a collection issue with a customer in Algeria, where the bank that was guaranteeing the debt of our customer was corrupt. And the officers of that bank ran away with all the money and left us holding the bag. We were able to engage the Commerce Department in having an ambassador go to bat for us in Algeria to try to recover that money. So that was a great benefit.

We also had issues with competitive deals in Morocco that looked like they were not so competitive, that maybe they had been wired for a particular vendor. And so we were able to exercise some consulting from the U.S. Commercial Service to have the ambassador also talk to the minister of communications there

Ex-Im Bank helps finance receivables.

and let him know that the U.S. was very interested in this particular deal. Just knowing that other people were watching kept that on the up-and-up and made it possible for us to win some business in Morocco.

It's kind of amazing that a small company in the U.S. could have all these ambassadors working on your behalf in foreign markets.

It's kind of amazing for me to think about as well. I never thought that kind of thing would happen, and it's flattering to get that kind of attention. And it's been good for us.

Do you have a favorite story of an experience that you had abroad where you were surprised by the way people did things and had an "Aha!" moment?

Maybe not so surprised. I mean, I think that a lot of cultures are very similar. There's a common ground that I see. That's really the "Aha!" moment for me—seeing how much in common I have with my counterparts in other cultures. And it's fascinating to learn their histories and why they govern themselves the way that they do, and learn about their different wars and battles and struggles. Just getting to know people is a fascinating part for me.

Do you have advice for small- and medium-sized enterprises, including manufacturers, about how to look at the world beyond the U.S.?

I'd say it's like anything else: Overcome your fear. Start with the thing that's going to be the least scary. So if you want to penetrate some markets overseas, start with people whose language you can understand. And we have a lot of language skills in the U.S., so there's people you can hire who have language skills that can also help you penetrate other markets. I'd say, "Don't be afraid." Take some initial steps. Take some initial orders. Don't get too risky all at once. Start small; grow from there. ∅

Bob Roche
Founder, CTRL Systems

Your company's literature says you are a nondestructive testing company. What then is a destructive testing company?

A destructive company would mean you'd have to tear something apart to do something productive. But in our case, it's ultrasound, nondestructive, allowing for diagnosis of leaky pipes while the equipment's still in motion.

What kinds of pipes do you work with, what do they leak, and why is it important to stop the leaks?

Pipes carrying compressed air, oil and gas, water. A leak is one of the applications of ultrasound. In the case of a leak, one of the main focuses that we provide for our clients globally is in the area of energy conservation, cost of energy. And one of the key ways of reducing costs is with compressed air. Compressed air historically has a wastage of 20 to 30 percent. So with our technology, [clients] can quickly locate and repair and confirm the repair and then reduce that consumption.

What kind of fluids or gases are passing through the pipes?

Just about any type. It can be a gas. It could be air; it could be any kind of medical gas. It can also be vacuum—be the reverse side. So in the case of our defense-related uses, they use it on the ships for the vacuum waste system.

How long have you been in operation, and how many staff do you have now?

The company was formed in 1989 and in about the mid-1990s we got involved in ultrasound, which was a diversion from what we originally were as a company. Since the mid-1990s, we have become a focused company on ultrasound technology. In the late 1990s we began doing exporting. We've been doing exporting since about '98.

And were you the brains behind the formation of the company?

I'm the founder.

What got you into this business? What was your background?

Happenstance. We were a computer-based company, maintenance software, and got involved with ultrasound from the original developer, realized its benefit and its opportunity, wound up acquiring the technology, then bringing in expertise and making it a very viable, competitive product in the market. One of our claims to fame is we put this technology on the International Space Station in 2001. NASA had been spending 8 years trying to do that. We helped them do it in 6 months.

Did you go up there yourself for the install?

No, I didn't get to go. In the case of, like, NASA, they use it for when they dock and the two doors come together. They can quickly scan and make sure they've got a good seal before they open the units. While on mission, it's been able to find failures onboard the space station. Some of the situations have been when they've been losing their internal oxygen out to space and they have to quickly find those problems and save this precious commodity of oxygen, which there's not a whole lot of in space.

How did the export side of the business get started?

I would like to say that it was a well laid out plan, but actually it was more of a too-dumb-to-know-that-you-couldn't-do-it. Our technology is a handheld diagnostic technology. It is cross-language in application, so. . . and of course English is a universal language for commerce, especially for engineers. So there was no barrier for us to deliver the product outside our borders. We began doing some export notification through the Internet, telling people "We export." We began working with the U.S. Department of Commerce and the Maryland Department of Economic Development and looked into some of the programs that could help us define possible partners in other countries. As a matter of fact, one of the partners that we started back in the 2000 time frame, which we were introduced to through the Department of Commerce and its local office in Baltimore, is still one of our clients today in Germany.

And some of our other international clients have come through Internet or other networking means; but we use a combination of promotion to export as well as other mechanisms that have brought partners. We sell our product around the world. Export now runs somewhere between 38 to 42 percent of our revenue stream. I'm a big believer in U.S. companies exporting and am on the Tech Council, which is a group of business participants mentoring other export companies on the export process.

And in just the last 3 years, since 2008, we have more than tripled our exporting volume, and this year we expect to see another appreciable growth in export contributions. So it's important to us, and it's important to us to help others understand exporting because, with the swings and turns of domestic business, the export business can be a hedge against the fluctuation. Fortunately for us last year—we do domestic, we do exporting and we do military—we were seeing growth in all three sectors, so it was very fortunate for us to have the best year we've had in a long time.

Has the export piece of it been helpful during the recession that we've had?

Yes, and I was going to say it's always been ever since we started a key element in the sustainment of the company and smoothing out fluctuations in other segments or other industry applications. We've been working in China for quite a while—3, 4 years now. We have sort of a pseudo-branch office in China. The press release we're putting out is that for the last 3 years, we've been doing a pilot program into their power industry, and we now have about 25 percent of their power plants using our technology.

The program just finished in 2011 and they've just reinstituted it for 2012 going forward. We expect to have probably about 40 percent penetration by the end of 2013. And probably within the next 2 to 3 years, close to 100 percent of the power plants will be using our technology on the power generation side. And that's a program sponsored by China's EPA.

> "... everything is both regional and timing, so something that we may have done successfully here can then be conveyed to another region of the world and they can replicate that success to their client's benefit, or vice versa."

We hear all kinds of not-very-positive things about doing business in China, one of which is the protection of intellectual property. How have you done that?

First of all, our product is protected through Intellectual Property (IP) and not through patent. Secondly, we develop relationships with partners that we feel as comfortable with as we can possibly be. Third, we have had companies try to reverse engineer our technology. They have reverse engineered the application but not the functionality and performance of our technology. So with that in mind, we're not fearful to go anywhere in the world, including China.

We're always cognizant of what could happen. But the other way to circumvent that too is always be innovating and always advancing your technology so that by the time someone maybe matches what you're currently doing, you are already onto the next or second version of the technology, advancing it to greater performance. So we don't let the pirating dissuade us from doing business.

Do you have a little R&D department in your company that is busy always trying to go up the innovation chain?

Yeah, we do; both for protection, as well as advancement of the technology to the benefit of the clients.

Are the machines made here in the U.S., or are they made elsewhere but have your software in them?

The handheld sensors are made here in the U.S. We have several subvendors that build components of ours and then we bring them together for final assembly and quality control, and then shipment from our facility to wherever they're going to go around the world. We also control our software, so final assembly and shipment goes out of our facility.

And the one interesting thing, from a commerce and offshore sourcing standpoint—3 to 4 years ago we wanted to take a couple of our components and reduce their cost of production. They were being machined and they lent themselves well to an injected-mold process. Within the U.S., the cost of the mold and the minimum quantities to do injected molding were still prohibitive for us to take that alternative. So about in the '07–'08 time frame, we wound up finding a source in China. And the production of the mold was more feasible. The small runs were more amenable to what we needed.

And we began doing that. About a year ago we were running into difficulties in communication about production runs. By being a small company and not having physical operations in country, the communication between ourselves and our offshore source had various challenges. And then we began looking back internally, and in the meantime—U.S. companies, being innovative in their situation—we have now pulled that back to the U.S.

We have now rebuilt the molds in the U.S. and we now have U.S. manufacturers producing our product in small, quick-run quantities that are both more in line with our needs and yet, at the same time, still at a price point that is lucrative for molding as opposed to milling. So I see it as a real success story, in general, of what has forced people to go offshore, but then bring it back into the U.S. So we're real happy with it.

And making things has all sorts of good, positive spinoffs in the local economy—the support that is required for trucking, the raw materials, and so forth.

Yes. Well, and the communication is a lot more convenient as well. No matter who you're dealing with, whether it's China or another part of the country, even though you do the best you can to be effective in what you're trying to convey, there are still challenges. And when you're a smaller company—that gets compounded. If you're a larger global organization, you may have means to do it better. We have 13 employees. We don't have a lot of depth for someone spending all their time on just that issue.

Can you give an example of how the U.S. government helped you accomplish a business goal that was meaningful?

One of our long-term partners in Germany was a group that we became aware of through the Department of Commerce and its Gold Key business matchmaking process. So in working with our team in Baltimore, laying out what we needed, what kind of partners we were looking for, they lined up several companies that had potential interest, we met with them and then formed a relationship with one company out of Munich and have been working with them since 2000. And they have a relationship with an engineering firm that has taken our technology and built it into a very specific application, allowing them to assess the condition of an automotive engine and assess the odometer reading as being accurate by the wear and tear of the engine or being fraudulent by someone modifying it. And they're doing quite well selling that in Western Europe and also in the Baltics.

In the Baltics it's a high percentage of vehicles that have the odometer tampered with, and so this technology—software algorithms using our ultrasound technology—is now giving them a new means to assess that and it's doing quite well. We just had them over recently, giving presentations to our Department of Transportation representatives and some others about the technology and how it's used for a very different purpose and need.

So the U.S. government here is actually contributing to your bottom line instead of subtracting from it.

I will say that we are using agencies within the government to facilitate our growth and help. And there have been individuals in various departments that have contributed in that, yes. So they're there to help, and when we ask for help they generally are very willing and able.

But like anything, you cannot expect to be the in-house representative and expect them to go off and do your work for you. You still have to convey your message, deliver your products and services to your clients, and uphold what it is that you've conveyed originally. But as far as networking and bringing possibilities, yeah, I think you can use them effectively.

What has your company learned in doing business overseas? Have the experiences that you've had made you a better engineer, a more effective and successful company?

What we learn is that everything is both regional and timing, so something that we may have done successfully here can then be conveyed to another region of the world and they can replicate that success to their client's benefit, or vice versa. A client overseas may be—just like the automotive situation—finding a niche for the technology, having deployed it with great success, and then bring that to other segments around the world. So that's more what we're learning—the interchangeability of success, best practices.

And because our technology is still relatively new and its applications are growing, 75 percent of the people that'll be using our technology in the next 5 years don't know it exists today. And therefore we're still in a large missionary mode of taking our technology into its application in many ways. So exchanging this information of success in various business and applications around the world is then helpful to then share it back around to other segments that hadn't even thought about it.

> *"I would like to say that [exporting] was a well laid out plan, but actually it was more of a too-dumb-to-know-that-you-couldn't-do-it.*

You're describing a kind of multiplier effect where you go—by virtue of being out there in the world and meeting these other companies who then have an "Aha!" moment, and then they apply it to something that you hadn't thought of before.
Correct.

This has a direct benefit to your bottom line.
Yes. And so then that's where the need stays tied to us, both to the IP and then the performance of the actual task at hand.

Have you had any interesting cultural interactions as you've gone around the world?
We were traveling and visiting various partners, and on one trip we were on our way to Brazil. And on the way to Brazil we were stopping off at Trinidad and Tobago. Maybe it was in 2000. We landed in Trinidad late at night, 11:30. We never had met the people that we were having our meetings with, but had phone conversations with them. And we're picked up, got in the car, introduced ourselves more formally and started to understand what was going on. And they informed us about the U.S. bombing of the aspirin facilities over in Africa, in a Muslim country. And they explained to us that they were Muslim.

That was a little moment of apprehension because we didn't know if world events were going to have any impact on our face-to-face visit. Happily to say, we had a very nice meeting, very cordial. We established business with them and all went well. But sometimes things going on around the world can catch up with you and can create an interesting moment.

It seems like you did not prejudge people by their cultural origins or religious beliefs, and that could have been the difference.

It was reciprocal on both sides. So it was a very good meeting; but again, during the announcement of the information, it created a little bit of pause to understand how we were going to be received.

As a member of your local Department of Commerce-sponsored District Export Council, you advise and mentor other companies that are interested in exporting. What is the single most important piece of advice that you can give these folks who come to you for counsel?

Anyone that I've talked to on behalf of that initiative, I just strongly suggest to them to give it real good consideration—that no matter what the size of the business, evaluation of the product being portable, and exportable without a lot of extra effort on their side, they should take the time to look into it. Since the U.S. Commercial Service office in Baltimore started the mentoring and training program a couple years ago, several people have been through it and they are now successfully exporting as well. A lot of times it's just a matter of a business owner not having the time to even think about it. So the important thing is to take the time to think about it. They'll be pleased with the return. ⬦

Steve Pope
Chief Marketing Officer, Domes International, Inc.

How did the company get started?

The company started in rural Mississippi in about 1993. The founder had been making chicken coops out of fiberglass and selling them to friends. The local undertaker, who doubled as the town's venture capitalist, bought one of the coops, saw the promise for other things besides chickens, and invested in the company. He got the operation out of the barn and into something resembling a factory. I came on as marketing director a couple of years later, and by then the main products were prefabricated fiberglass structures. They seemed right for developing countries in need of efficient, inexpensive housing. So we became Domes International, Inc., manufacturers of structures made of molded fiberglass. Yes, I suppose some of them do look like igloos, others like marshmallows. But among the most attractive benefits of fiberglass domes is their low maintenance. They're termite resistant and energy efficient, they also protect against dangerous weather conditions, including severe monsoons that cause terrible damage and loss of life in certain areas of the world. Millions of people are born every day, and they all need housing.

How did you make the decision to expand globally from the founder's original product line and rural market?

When Domes International decided to expand internationally, we were already selling houses to the U.S. military for bases on tropical islands. I became director of international business development and marketing. I was also president of World Discoveries, Inc., an export-import and international manufacturing and marketing consulting company based in Memphis. The company contracted with Domes for its global manufacturing operations.

The challenge for us was to select the best markets and find buyers. For that we turned to the government in the form of the U.S. Commercial Service offices in Memphis, Tennessee, and Jackson, Mississippi. After talking with trade specialists at the centers, we decided to focus on India. The combined forces of the U.S. Commercial Service in Mumbai, Delhi, and in the U.S. provided us with market research and help on doing business with the Indian government, including contacts within the government who might be interested in purchasing domes. Those contacts included officials from Gujarat State who needed to house thousands of homeless families. The State placed an order, and later the Indian military did as well.

We soon realized that we needed a facility in India to assemble components shipped from the U.S. Having a local facility is a win-win because jobs created help the local economy, while we benefit stateside by providing the higher end components. The U.S. Commercial Service then helped us apply for a $1,200,000 U.S. government-backed loan from the Overseas Private Investment Corporation (OPIC). That was in 2003. Then, when the first shipment of the fiberglass molds and machinery got hung up in customs, Commercial Service officials helped retrieve them and arranged for operating permits and inspection protocols. Additionally, the U.S. Commercial Service offices in Mumbai, New Delhi, and Ahmedabad, India, helped obtain some necessary product registration certificates from the Indian Ministry of Commerce. This was amazing because there's no way we could have done these things from thousands of miles away.

These early experiences led to more sales as we adapted the product to fit local needs. Domes can be used as offices, schools, military barracks, and warehouses. A religious group in Western India replaced more expensive marble temples with fiberglass domes. You never know what new opportunities might arise when you're on the ground observing what people need.

In another case, a government client for a school building pointed out that people in one part of the state considered round structures with a hole in them as kind of a temple of doom and gloom. Local folks wouldn't go near them. So we developed flat fiberglass panels and added ribs and steel struts for strength. It became a more acceptable box, not a dome. So we opened our factory in Ahmedabad and began selling houses, schoolrooms, and warehouses in the surrounding area.

Then things didn't turn out as planned.

They didn't. The Indian business partner became ill. Then the price of oil, from which fiberglass comes, doubled, making the product more expensive for buyers. The local market not only wasn't as robust as thought, but it began to go south. Then the U.S. economy tanked. I think it was mostly bad luck and timing, but the venture wasn't doing well and we ended up selling it to an Indian buyer. That was in January 2012, 9 years after we got the OPIC loan and opened the factory. What we learned the hard way is that your partners have to have sufficient cash reserves and you need sufficient up-front orders to put the business on a good footing. Of course, some luck would help, too. So we've been licking our wounds.

But you're still pursuing new ventures.

Yes, we hope to close a deal soon in Turkey, and we're negotiating others. We're looking at potential deals in Africa and the Middle East. There's a big demand out there, and we have a good solution. We haven't been idle. We're improving what we have. We've improved the way we make the product, lowering our costs. We learned to reinforce the composite wall panels after a jail break from one of our structures in Alabama. The inmates dug their way out with a spoon!

Other than the importance of picking good joint venture partners, what else have you learned?

You have to be flexible. Our initial business plan was based on the then-current oil prices. The company's raw materials are 70 percent petroleum based. We went to India expecting to sell lots of single-family homes, and by the time we finally opened our factory oil prices had doubled, and hence our raw materials as well. We discovered the better market was local governments and the military. We had to go there, make this discovery, then adjust on the fly.

There's no doubt that Domes International is a better company as a result of our experience in India. We are much more flexible and also innovative. The client wanted a less expensive structure, so we went back to our labs and came up with an insulation solution that met their needs. Now we use these discoveries to improve core products and to offer more variations. We are much more confident going into new situations—listening, adapting, and finding the best solution. That we've been able to transform through our experiences overseas in just a few years is amazing. In retrospect, setting up a factory in another country is a whole different kettle of fish. We probably should have found an existing factory that could have modified some of its capacity to custom build our structures. This would have been much cheaper than building from scratch. We took a gamble building an overseas facility instead of supplying demand as it arose from the U.S. We won't shy away from producing again in a foreign market, but we'll insist on very different selection criteria from the partner. We'll also have a more realistic sense of the extra time needed to deal with the local governments and to have the staying power needed to succeed in these markets. ⌀

Charles Popenoe III
Owner, SmartBolts

How did you get into this business?

My father worked for the National Institute of Standards and Technology as a scientist. And in his spare time, as a hobby, he was an inventor. He still is an inventor. And he invented the SmartBolt and patented it.

How did he do it? In his garage or his basement?

Garage, basement, both.

And he just tinkered around, and there it is.

He saw an article in *Popular Science* about a bolt with a little glass window that breaks when you tighten it to the proper tension. And so he said, "Well, that's neat, but I can come up with a better idea than that." And he worked and worked and actually took 10 or 15 years to develop it to a state that it could be marketable.

As an engineering problem it probably was pretty daunting.

It depends on a fluid. The fluid is what makes the color change. And what type of fluid, and what were the qualities of the fluid, and how to contain the fluid were really the biggest challenges; he really had to innovate.

How are the bolts used?

The applications are numerous. But we've had one in particular that's caught on, and it's really caught on worldwide. It's our most successful application. It's used for electrical connections. And basically you're joining conducting bars and they're carrying current, and they've got to be tight, or else you get heat buildup and the potential of arc, and other issues. The bus bars need an important bolt to hold them together to prevent heat buildup; and it's easy for inspection as well, because you can just look at the bolt and know that it's properly tightened without touching those high-current-carrying bars. So GE originally pioneered the use of our bolt about 15 years ago for this application. And by doing so, they made a market for us where we've been able to expand into other manufacturers of the same product, both in the U.S. and globally.

How about critical things that, if they fall off, would cause severe problems for the people who are riding or flying in them?

Yes. Actually, we have a customer who's an amusement park ride manufacturer. And they even export those rides, as a matter of fact, with our bolts, which hold them together and make them easy to inspect to determine that the bolts are properly tensioned.

How many employees do you have, and how many of these bolts can they generate?

We have six employees, including myself: four people in manufacturing and then two in sales and marketing. Our capacity is about 75,000 pieces a year. That's up from 25,000 last year, so we're growing pretty dramatically.

And these bolts are made not in Asia, but in the U.S., right?

Yes. We normally start with the ordinary bolt, and then we machine it and modify it and insert our indicator to become a tension-indicating SmartBolt. And this bolt was actually made entirely in the U.S.—even the steel, the bolt cold heading, and then all our work.

> "... we're strong on search terms like 'tension-indicating bolts,' 'torque-indicating bolts.' And we get a lot of interest from overseas on our website

When did you start selling outside the U.S.?

We were really were just focusing on the U.S. We got a few inquiries from overseas. And one that we cultivated was with a Turkish company which is very similar to GE, but operating in Turkey. It was for the same application. I think it was 2009 when we got our first big order from them. At that point, the people we were working with suggested that I talk to the U.S. Commercial Service to help us get started in our exporting program.

Have there been additional countries since the sales to Turkey?

Yes. Our sales to Turkey are ongoing, so we've been able to keep that customer happy. But we're also selling to Taiwan. We have a new agreement with a company in Australia to sell throughout Southeast Asia. We're selling to South Africa, Japan, Korea, and the list goes on. Really, any industrial country could use our products. We plan to just keep on growing to meet the demand, keeping our sales growing, introducing new products that are complementary and making advances in the technology.

> "It feels good to be exporting to other countries and the positive role the U.S. can play in the world."

What else have you got there? It looks like a nutcracker.

This is our demonstrator product. Basically this shows you what will happen when we tighten the bolt. You can see that it's red when it's loose, and when you tighten it it's black.

So you can instantly see whether it's loose or tight by looking at the indicator. Actually you can judge intermediate tensions as well.

How did the U.S. government help you expand overseas?

We learned from a customer about a program called ExporTech. And we enrolled in that right away. It turns out it was just starting. And it was a very valuable program to help us get our export program going.

What is ExporTech?

ExporTech helps small companies determine if they have a good product for export, and then gives them all the tools they need to know about the financing, harmonized tariff codes, taxes, all sorts of nuts-and-bolts operational things you need to know to be able to export. We learned a tremendous amount from that program. It really helped us complete that sale to the Turkish company and to execute it successfully. So it helped us get our first big sale done. And then that just made it possible for us to progress from there. We met the Turks through our GE customer, which shows that you may already be selling to a domestic customer who can help you sell to one of their international customers, if you ask. ExporTech was just opening a door to the varied services that the U.S. Commercial Service provides. From that point, one of the outputs of the ExporTech program was being able to

> "We're selling to South Africa, Japan, Korea, and the list goes on."

create a business plan to submit to the State of Maryland for an Export MD grant, which helps pay for some our international sales efforts. And that led to a Trade Winds trade mission to Brazil that we did the following year. So it's really been a series of services and facilities that have become available to us. They've all helped.

What are the main components of the export plan?

It's really identifying our market. But I think one of the key things we got out of the ExporTech program is that this is an outstanding product for export—because it's high value, it's unique, it's the kind of thing that can be used in almost any industrial nation. And so that was the foundation of our plan: we have a very good product for export and we have to treat the international market very seriously if we want to grow.

> "…it's been exciting and motivating to our employees to know that a product is going to Taiwan, for example."

What else have you done to find international customers?

We have a good Internet presence and website, and we're strong on search terms like "tension-indicating bolts," "torque-indicating bolts." And we get a lot of interest from overseas on our website.

Would it surprise you to know that the majority of inquiries that come to U.S. companies from overseas via the Internet go unanswered?

It would surprise me, because believe me, we answer all of ours!

Do you have anything on your website that is helpful for the international buyer? Do you indicate that you ship internationall?

I think that's something we could probably do more with, really. yWe don't have much in the way of any other language capability. So I think it's the visual nature of the product. And we have demonstrations—animations that help people easily grasp what's happening. But we do depend on some understanding of the English language as well.

> "I personally enjoy working with people from other countries and learning about their backgrounds and their cultures."

Have orders actually come from the exposure of the product via the Internet?

Yes. It's leads that we develop. But we've been able to develop them without travel: mostly by email—and telephone occasionally—but mostly by email.

You've made significant sales to foreign markets without actually having to go there.

Right, with a couple of exceptions. I'm actually going to Istanbul next month to visit my Turkish customer. So they've become a very important part of our business, and so it's about time I visited them. We've made a couple of other overseas visits. But we have been dependent on them to get our business.

Try the rice pudding. It's really delicious.

Sounds great. Looking forward to it.

"At that point, the people we were working with suggested that I talk to the U.S. Commercial Service to help us get started in our exporting program."

Well really, ExporTech was just opening a door to the varied services that the U.S. Commercial Service provides. From that point, one of the outputs of the ExporTech program was being able to create a business plan to submit to export—to the State of Maryland for an Export MD grant, which helps pay for some of our international sales efforts. And that actually led to a Trade Winds mission to Brazil that we did the following year. So it's really been a series of services and facilities that have kind of made— become available to us. They've all helped, really.

How do you protect your intellectual property in the markets you are operating in?

It is patented. And we have a series of patents, some international. But mostly we're protecting it based on the fact that we're the only ones that know how to make it, and it's not trivial to manufacture, and we're trying to stay ahead of the competition.

It took your dad 10 years to develop it so this would be hard to reverse engineer it in short order.

Yes. But at the same time, we know that the challenge is there. And then we have to keep developing new products to stay ahead of those who would copy it.

What's on the docket for new things? Can you share with us what you're working on now that you hope to bring to market?

We have a product we're developing that's a high-resolution model that's more sensitive than this model. We also have a product we're developing on which you can read the color without any light source or any visual.

By getting out of the U.S. and dealing with people with different backgrounds in different parts of the world, have you been able to learn and apply things that have helped your company grow, become maybe more competitive or more innovative?

It's great to understand that there's a market for our product internationally and try to meet customers' requirements. I personally enjoy working with people from other countries and learning about their backgrounds and their cultures. And it's been exciting and motivating to our employees to know that a product is going to Taiwan, for example. It feels good to be exporting to other countries and the positive role the U.S. can play in the world.

What percentage of your business now is international?

Last year about 50 percent of our sales were international. So it's significant, very significant. It may even be greater than that this year.

What advice would you have for other U.S. companies that are considering expanding internationally or getting into it for the first time?

Certainly the local U.S. Commercial Service office has a lot of resources to help companies determine whether they're a good candidate for exporting. And I think that's where I would start, because that will point companies in the right direction to see where they should go from there, and whether they should consider if exporting should be a big part of their sales and marketing plan.

"We learned a tremendous amount from that program. It really helped us complete that sale to the Turkish company and to execute it successfully."

You're enthusiastic about your role in exporting. Have you been able to share this sense of enthusiasm and possibility with other manufacturing companies that are not exporting now, but that you have contact with in the Baltimore area?

I've been doing that somewhat. And I think one of the great things about the U.S. Commercial Service is the opportunity to network and to meet others that are similar to us that are exporting— either as a role model for us or, at some point, we become the role model for others. At this point we're a fledgling exporter. But, you know, in the future I certainly hope to be a model and assist others in the same path.

Fifty percent is hardly fledgling, but I admire your understatement and your modesty.

Well, we're still a small company. But we're growing. ⬦

Maria de Lourdes Sobrino
Founder, LuLu's Dessert

How did the business get started?

It all began in 1982 in a 700-square-foot storefront in Torrance, California, with a milk crate for a chair and my mother's Mexican-style recipe for gelatin. Some friends joined me in preparing tasty treats—and soon I started my own company, LuLu's Dessert. LuLu is my nickname. Many of the recipes are snacks from my childhood, such as jalapeño-flavored carrots and roasted peanuts. Then I started making jiggly fruit-flavored taste treats known in Spanish as *gelatina*. Unlike Jell-O, which then was made only in powdered form, my gelatin was ready to eat from the time a customer bought it—a concept that Jell-O would not market for another 11 years.

With gelatins such as Fruit Fantasia, Orange Blast, Creamy Vanilla with Cinnamon, and Sugar Free-De-Light, we have something for everyone. With total sales this year of $6 million, we're doing a good business in the U.S. and Mexico. We began exporting to Mexico in 1992 and opened offices and a distribution center there, but despite our knowledge of the Mexican market we faced great difficulty in selling there because of our inexperience in the export process. I often had only vague information on potential distributors of our product and did not know how to ensure that they were qualified and legitimate. I also did not have the most updated market research reports on Mexico. Time passed and we began to learn the ropes of international trade. We've been in business for 30 years now and are about to partner with some very large supermarkets in Mexico. I'm hoping they'll take delivery at our factory and handle all the logistics themselves.

What have been your big challenges?

The domestic economy was very bad, especially in 2008 and 2009. We kept the doors open and all 25 of us employed, but it was really hard. We really got squeezed by the cost of everything and weak demand. At some point we decided to move the factory to Texas and will do so this year. Texas is a better location, as it's close to central Mexico while also situated to more economically serve the U.S. West and East coasts where a lot of Hispanic people live. We also looked at Oklahoma, Nevada and Arizona. Texas seems better for our business goals. Another factor was the price of gas. It really adds a lot to the cost of goods. Then there are all the high overhead costs in Southern California. Margins are squeezed and there's nothing left for expansion or product development. Then there are the banks, or lack of them. I grew the business based on loans and lines of credit. Everything froze during the recession. The banks seem uninterested in small business. What they care about are profits and big numbers. They pretend to loan. It's really hard for a profitable business to borrow $500,000 to try new things, develop new products. Everyone talks about how important small business is, how many jobs small business creates. But a lot of it is just talk. When we get to Texas, which is offering incentives to move there, we'll take more advantage of free-trade agreements and expand in Mexico and also into Central America, where food preferences are similar.

What are some of the lessons you've learned?

The biggest lesson learned early on was not to try to do it alone when it comes to exporting. When I began exporting, I had no idea that government resources, the Export-Import Bank, were available. I spent 10 years trying to make international sales and continued to run into all kinds of problems—especially buyers who wouldn't pay or couldn't afford letters of credit. One time I even went to Chile to try to collect a debt from a customer, but had no luck. By using Export-Import Bank services that provide background checks on potential partners and letters of credit to guarantee payment, I have much more confidence in doing business with foreign partners. The success of LuLu's Dessert in foreign markets has been boosted by the assistance of the Western U.S. Agricultural Trade Association (WUSATA), which has provided money for marketing outside the U.S. The funds gave me the opportunity to travel, to participate in trade shows, and to create brochures targeted to overseas markets while being reimbursed a large percentage by WUSATA. It's really a good program and helps us compete. I also benefited from the U.S. Commercial Service's customized market research reports much earlier in my export endeavors. U.S. companies also need to be diligent about trademark protection, because in one European country the LuLu's trademark was stolen and used by another company.

I also found that customers abroad often prefer sweeter desserts than do people in the U.S. So you need to research these differences and change the product so that it meets the customers' preferences. When it comes to exporting, don't do everything by yourself. When I go out to speak, I give businesses a good lesson in exporting.

After reading an article about me in a local newspaper, Tony Michalski, a trade specialist at the U.S. Commercial Service office in Newport Beach, California, contacted me to see how he could help me realize our exporting goals. Tony provided services such as export counseling and market research. We really started to make progress. I was put in touch with organizations such as the California Trade and Commerce Agency and the U.S. Agricultural Trade Office. As a result, LuLu's Dessert began to have greater success in foreign markets, especially Mexico. Today, we compete with local food manufacturers in Mexico, having contracts at grocery chains like Wal-Mart and Oxxo and an exclusive distributorship in the Mexican state of Baja California. The HEB grocery chain, with stores in

Texas and Mexico, may become a big customer for us. We'll have much more space, more production machines, and can expand our production of rice pudding and flan. We'll need more workers.

Won't it be difficult to leave California after all this time and all the memories?

Oh, it will be a huge change! We have so many colleagues and friends, along with a pretty big extended family. But I love this business. A lot of people might have given up after what we've been through. I don't want to give up. I want to try new things, find new opportunities. I look forward to a new chapter in Texas. Exporting accounts for about 5 percent of the company's total revenues, but with a greater production capacity and more products, I can grow the company even more, especially internationally. We think that all the world deserves one of our treats.

What are the contacts you'll want to preserve in California?

One is the Technology Entrepreneurship and Cultural Mexican Association of Orange County. That's a mouthful, but it brings together businesspeople and artists on both sides of the border to meet each other and to do business. Chapman College in Orange, California, has been a main patron, and sponsors an annual event which I attend. Networking is an important aspect of getting new business and customers. You never know where they'll come from next, but you need to be proactive. Mexico will remain one of our most important trading partners.

What changes have you seen in Mexico?

Of course I love Mexico because I was born there and still have family. There have been huge changes there—most for the better. The president has done a good job with the economy. They've discovered more offshore oil. The middle class will grow richer, and they will travel and buy more U.S. goods and services. This will drive the economies of Central America. So business should be good there for a long time. I'm moving my whole company closer to take advantage of these opportunities. ◊

Richard Brenner
CEO, Amarr Garage Doors

How did the company get started?

It's a typical immigrant story. My grandfather and his three brothers came over from what is now Latvia in the 1950s. The brothers started dozens of different businesses. One of them was Amarr, which is a play on the names of two of the brothers—Abe and Morris. My dad was the only brother to attend college. He was one of only two Jews at The Citadel, a military school. He lasted a year and transferred to a state college. Amarr began selling other manufacturers' doors, then moved to installing them and finally to making our first wood doors in 1969.

David Reed, Director of International Sales (left); Richard A. Brenner, CEO (right)

So you had business in your bones. But what about international?

As kids we had the connection with Europe. I suppose another ingredient is that my mother's brother was a Harvard professor who coined the term globalization. We heard that a lot growing up, and now we're doing it. It's really a mind-set, and we see selling to, and engaging with, the world as a mind-set that looks at things as why not? Versus why?

Can you tell us what challenges you faced in getting into the international marketplace?

The international arena posed a lot of significant challenges for us. First was the understanding that a garage door for the U.S. is not the same as a garage door internationally. So, being able to customize our product to international specifications was the first. Then there were also international certifications to obtain, particularly CE certification for Europe. And we also had a lot of challenges just through things getting lost in translation.

Like what, for example?

Well, I think one of the big things is understanding meaning when you're working internationally, and if your customer doesn't speak English everything takes three times longer. You speak; it's translated. They speak; it's translated. So just having the stamina in negotiations is actually one big thing. You have to be patient because significant sales don't materialize overnight. What looks like an overnight success can be years in the making.

What was the payoff for having stamina and patience?

We sell to about 30 countries right now and have distributors in most of them. Volume does not exceed our U.S. domestic sales, but is an important part of the mix and has created many new jobs in our company. Our international sales actually grew when our U.S. sales didn't during the 2008–2009 recession. That helped us a lot. Our number one international market is the European Union. And while growth has slowed there recently, Europe is not the whole world. Another kind of stamina involves food adventures. Recently, a Norwegian customer wanted to treat us to something very special: eating sheep's heads. And then after having to eat this disgusting thing, which is a very important tradition to them, they had to go show us how they were actually made. So we think we can leave it at that.

Was there a big difference between going from that first international sale to additional ones in more country markets?

No. I think it was just a little bit of an iteration difference. So once you understand the first one it really helps you to getting to the next one. As the international began to grow we made a strategic decision to hire an international marketing specialist and to build a little team around this person to generate more growth. We hired him in the early 1990s to get us into Mexico, which he did very successfully. He's one of a thousand people who work at Amarr.

How long did it take to go from one to many?

Over 20 years, as our first export was to Australia in the 1980s. So it takes time to build your brand and to build the fact that we are an internationally thinking company, not just a domestic producer that happens to be opportunistic to export; but we had to dedicate resources and time to it.

How did you become an "international-thinking" company?

It's a mind-set. It's something I was interested in. I thought it was important for our business. There's only 320 million people in the U.S., and there's a lot more internationally. So it's just a matter of focus. Successful exporting is focus versus fine line. Fine line was the one-off shipment to Australia in the 1980s. Focus was Australia 10 years later when we hired specialized staff, made use of U.S. government export promotion services, and developed networks of distributors. There are different levels involved as part of a process. The first level is to sell internationally. The next level is to make the commitment to international sales by adding resources. The third is to strategically plan entry into each country market.

What effect has being an international company had on the company, including you, the CEO—other than the sheep's heads, of course?

"It's really a mind-set, and we see selling to, and engaging with, the world as a mind-set that looks at things as why not? Versus why?"

Being an exporter has made us a better company domestically and internationally. I think we're better listeners to the needs of our domestic customers by understanding what's done internationally. And our international dealers have taught us things about what they see in their market that we've translated back to our market. So it's broadened our scope. Our practice now is to send our U.S.-based engineers to the new international market to talk with engineers there. Our engineers return from these meetings brimming with enthusiasm and ideas for improving current products and creating new ones.

Is there one example that you could give us of something that you imported back to the U.S. that helped you be more competitive in all markets—something that you learned?

When we were going through our CE testing we learned some things through that process with an international dealer of ours and an international parts distributor that we brought back—because we do a lot of wind-load testing here in the U.S., and we're able to bring that learning back and help reduce some costs and create a higher wind-loaded product for our markets here. Recently, we opened an R&D lab as part of our company. Now we can certify ourselves for internal markets and certify the products of other U.S. companies by testing them in our lab. We got this idea from our international business.

How do you find international customers?

We look at markets in terms of per-capita income. For the residential doors, we look at how people feel about their automobiles. There are surveys available. In Europe, car care is hugely important, and one way to care for your car is to have a good garage and a secure garage door. So people might not have money to spend on other things, but they will spend it on cars and car care. But customers can come from anywhere. We get a lot of business by attending international trade shows in the building industry. Sometimes it's luck. I was at a trade show recently, when I was introduced to somebody who liked the product and bought a container load.

Was that luck or part of your strategy of going to these markets? Was it luck that put you at that trade show in that country?

I guess it was both. You've got to get out there. We have a good website, but that's not where we sell doors. We sell them to distributors who we find and select based on what we call our "Culture of Caring Service." We also engage the U.S. government in helping us find distributors.

"The first level is to sell internationally. The next level is to make the commitment to international sales by adding resources. The third is to strategically plan entry into each country market."

Can you tell us a little bit about how the government helped you?

Alan Richel of the Commerce Department's Houston office has been very instrumental in helping us overcome barriers in certain markets where we needed some help, not only through connections, but just through education on things that we and our international sales team needed.

Have they helped you in the Middle East and in China?

Yes, and we have and continue to sell doors in China. I would say probably going to China and seeing Western-style subdivisions where they were trying to replicate various styles of homes that we might find here in the West. McMansions I just found to be very, very amusing. Interest in these designs continues, but our growth in China has not met expectations because the Chinese are making their own doors now. That could change, and I'm talking to a potential Chinese customer today. The Chinese are patient people. We can learn from them.

What advice would you give people who are contemplating exporting or exporting beyond one or a few markets?

I would say three things. First of all, dedicate your mind to the fact that this is something you want to be involved in. Then dedicate the resources in terms of people and money. And then also get help from the U.S. Department of Commerce and other government agencies. ∅

Rosie Herman
Founder, Mykytyn Enterprises Inc.

You were the subject of a tabloid headline when your business started out.

Yes, the headline said "Penniless Mom Strikes It Rich." It pretty much summed up my story and the nail and hand care business I created from everyday ingredients in my kitchen. I'd been a salon owner and manicurist for 15 years in Houston, Texas. I had expensive fertility treatments that put me into debt. I gave birth to twin girls, and at that point my goal was to be a stay-at-home mom. That phase didn't last long, and I was soon in my kitchen mixing natural ingredients into lotions to fix "lizard skin"—hands cracked and bleeding from too much cooking, cleaning, and caregiving. The recipe was a little bit of this and a little bit of that. I sold the mixture, which includes grapefruit, peppermint, spearmint, avocado, rosemary, and apricot, to some local salons, and soon they were clamoring for more. My husband, who's also my business partner, renamed the product the One Minute Manicure, which made marketing easier.

Business took a leap when I gave a manicure to Oprah Winfrey on *The Oprah Winfrey Show* and was featured in *People Magazine* and a tabloid as the former "penniless mom." The *Oprah Winfrey Show* is syndicated worldwide, and I got, and still get, email inquiries and orders from Australia, the Netherlands, and other countries. Celebrities Billy Joel and Jenna Elfman also provided endorsements.

What was your big challenge 15 years ago?

I realized that I had a product for which there was interest beyond the U.S. But my company, named for my husband, Mykytyn Enterprises Inc., was a small family startup business. I wondered how I'd navigate the world of commerce. The world is awash in beauty products. How would mine stand out? With the help of my sister-in-law, who knew stuff about international marketing, we lined up distributors outside the country. International sales were a priority from the start because they offered faster growth and greater efficiencies. In just a few years I had formed an international network of 200 distributors. International sales for the company, with its 12 full-time employees plus production staff, were about 20 percent of total earnings when we talked 6 years ago. Now they are 40 to 60 percent. I've developed a product that does not require a lot of modification because of consumer or cultural differences. Looking and feeling good is a universal desire.

Does that mean there are no cultural differences?

Well, in France women prefer pineapple scent, while in the U.S. women like pomegranate. Other differences include labeling. The European Union now wants every single ingredient on the label, and they've announced a ban on paraben, a preservative used in some beauty products, but not in our signature One Minute Manicure. Luckily, they've given everyone 18 months for the labeling change so that inventories can run down before the change becomes official.

What was your experience entering the French market, which is part of the EU?

We've had our distributor in France for many years who's great. He said in an email to me: "You are seducing the French, which is not an easy task." We've relied on him to teach us about consumer preferences. Business is a little slow in France right now, so he's reaching out to some other European markets. We are also doing well in Mexico, the Netherlands, and the United Kingdom. A distributor in Peru placed an order for $10,000, and South Korea has welcomed the product. We've also sent our first container to our distributor in South Africa.

Is there anything different about selling there?

The distributor has used my personal story to build brand recognition. Women there identify with struggle, leading to ultimate success. Generally, we've found that many women appreciate small, specialty producers as opposed to the megabrands. We've used this insight to help distributors position the product. I'd like to go to South Africa and do some media to promote the product.

What other insights have contributed to your business?

Doing business in Europe gives us a sense of where European regulations and consumer protection are going. What we do in terms of product labeling in Europe, we'll do in the U.S. and elsewhere. Learning about customer preferences has made us more sensitive to them, and to the importance of asking questions and working with local distributors with an open mind. The Internet is a great place to find new customers. Getting the right provider for our site has been a challenge—we're on our third now. We have links to all of our distributors on the site and insist that the distributors have their own sites with our branding. So we refer business directly to them, just as we get expressions of interest from potential distributors in new markets. The biggest insight is that we need to be active in international markets. If it weren't for international sales, we wouldn't have survived the recession, especially the worst of it in 2008 and 2009. The international markets saved us.

China?

We've been trying, but haven't found the right distributors yet. Payment has been an issue.

Hasn't all this success created envy and knockoffs around the world?

Yes. At one point, there were 50 different variations of the One Minute Manicure, some with remarkably similar packaging and branding. But none provided much competition for our product. Certainly none were as good. Only a handful remain—and they probably won't survive.

What's your experience working with government export assistance programs?

We love them. In particular, I've worked with the U.S. Commercial Service office in Houston. In addition to finding distributors, the U.S. Commercial Service trade specialists provide background checks on prospective buyers, many of whom are coming to us through our website. A buyer in India ordered $400,000 worth of product. But a U.S. Commercial Service trade specialist ran a background check and discovered that all the information provided, including the bank account numbers, was phony. You just have to do your homework and make use of the government export assistance programs that are available. After I was on the Oprah show I received hundreds of emails from women wanting to start or expand their own businesses. I told them to think globally and contact the U.S. Commercial Service for help getting there.

Do you have a lodestar for your business?

I follow the Three P's: Passion, Perseverance, and Patience. In other words, follow your dream; don't accept "no" for an answer; be patient and tackle one problem at a time. You should always ask for assistance and advice when engaging in international business. Don't try to do it alone.

Are your twin daughters interested in the business?

They do help out at peak times, but they're only 14, so it's early to see what their future interests are. They are very busy in school. That's good because to remain competitive, our country needs a great educational system, especially in the lower grades. ∅

William Haynes
Founder, Sabai Technology

How did you get started?

It actually started when I got laid off. After looking for work for a couple of months I decided to put some of my knowledge to use and started developing specialized routers. There's always been a big users' group of alternative firmware called DD-WRT or Tomato, and what I found was there were people who wanted to use this technology—this firmware—on their routers but maybe didn't have the same technical background that I did. So I started developing these for shipping domestically, and the next step was looking for companies that use these types of routers, but that's not their business, that's not what they're selling.

And in looking for that, the first company I found is a company called HotSpot Systems, that does those hotspot routers that are in airports and travel places. And I started shipping routers for them, configured for their services. The next partner company we found was a company called StrongVPN. They provide VPN services— virtual private network services. Say you're an executive who's been assigned to China for 2 years, but you still want access, and you want secure access to the U.S. StrongVPN provides those VPN services so that you can connect to the U.S. and all your Internet traffic is encrypted from China to the U.S., and then once it hits the U.S. it goes out to the open Internet and goes to its target. There were a lot of people who wanted routers to do that for their whole household rather than just one computer so we contacted that company and asked them if we could develop routers for their customers. They agreed, and next thing you know we were shipping internationally.

Who does the engineering stuff?

I've worn every hat here, as any entrepreneur will tell you. I've just hired people smarter than me in those areas that can do the software programming and things like that. I'm more the bigger picture guy. I can get into the details, but I have to be highly focused: the door's got to be shut and people have to leave me alone kind of stuff. But in terms of knowing what I want the customer experience to be or knowing what I want the operating system to look like or knowing how I want it to work to meet what the needs of the customer are: that's more my role as we grow.

Did you have a rough time in the tough economy?

I started last year, it was just me—employee number one. I couldn't have picked a better time—even though it's a tough time economically for people. I got help when I was unemployed until I got things up and going. The business gets tax incentives for the new people I hire. The Department of Commerce comes in and holds my hand and works with me on finding new customers around the world. There's just resource after resource after resource that I couldn't have imagined. And I'm honored beyond words to be able to employ those people that I'm providing with an income and a career.

William Haynes holding a Sabai router.

How many countries are you now selling product to?

We sell product to every country except the ones that the Department of Commerce has told us not to and then there's a list that they've asked us to check with them before we ship. But we have currently shipped to about 80 countries. We have about nine full- and part-time employees.

That's extraordinary, considering the typical U.S. exporter ships to a handful of countries at the most.

We've shipped to some incredibly interesting places. We did a lot of business in the Middle East during the spring because of the spring uprising.

The Arab Spring.

Yes, the Arab Spring—a lot of people wanted unfettered access to news and information, and our router helped make that possible. So we were shipping a lot to many of those countries this spring. But one of my favorites is we shipped to the Faroe Islands. It was there, I think, in 3 or 4 days. And if you're not familiar with where the Faroe Islands are, they're halfway between Iceland and Scotland, out in the middle of nowhere.

Without getting into the technical aspects of your device, when you shipped these routers to the Middle East during the Arab Spring, your device helps private citizens, for example, get around whatever governmental-imposed blackouts there might be in that area?

Yeah, it basically encrypts. Say an executive or someone who's bought our router has it in their home or business. Everything from their network—all their computers and devices that connect to our router—it's unencrypted within the home, but as soon as it hits the router, the router encrypts it and there are two different levels—a low level of encryption or a high level, depending on the security and speed that the person needs. And it takes it encrypted from that home all the way to the endpoint that the user has chosen where their server is—so either the U.S., or if someone's a UK citizen they might have a server in the UK.

So it stays encrypted until it hits that endpoint server, at which point it's decrypted and goes out to the Internet. So it allows people—like during the Arab Spring—to go to CNN and get the news and information; to send emails knowing that from the time it leaves their home to the time it hits the U.S. or the country they're connected to, it's totally encrypted so that they can send an email asking for information. Now once it hits the U.S. server or whatever it's connecting to, at that point it's decrypted and just regular Internet traffic like you would send over your ISP.

Doesn't some encrypted technology require a license from the U.S. government before it can be exported?

Yes, but not the kind we sell.

How would you describe the importance of exporting to your company? What percentage of sales does it comprise now?

Oh my goodness. I would say, at this point, 85 percent of our routers are going overseas.

And what's made this possible is the leap in logistics. The experience for the end customer is excellent. We had a customer who ordered at 2:34 in the afternoon on a Monday from São Paulo, Brazil. Well, 10 a.m. on Wednesday morning—less than 48 hours later, they're contacting us letting us know they've gotten the router, it's installed, it's up—"Thank you so much, how wonderful this is." Any small company can take advantage of these shipping solutions, the online tools, and so much more.

. . to have someone hold my hand a bit and walk me through it—it's going to really accelerate the rate at which we can grow our international business."

What kind of help did you receive from the government?

For me—for a new business—and for someone who isn't that knowledgeable—I'm gaining knowledge every day in exports. The biggest thing was that the local Department of Commerce people came and sat with me; we went through my company specifically. So it wasn't a generalized conversation about exporting; it was our exporting at Sabai Technology—what we're doing, where we're selling to. And we discussed basically the resources that were available. One of the things that we did was—advertise in a magazine called *Commercial News USA*. It goes out monthly with opportunities for people in other countries to become distributors or partners with companies. So we have advertised in that and we've gotten interest from, and selected companies, in countries like Zambia wanting to buy and distribute our product.

A lot of the help is just information I wouldn't have even known. A Commerce rep discussed with me how you can insure your product when it's being shipped and you're ensuring that you're going to receive the funds from the other party, how letters of credit work. I'm just a babe in the woods with this stuff, and to have someone hold my hand a bit and walk me through it—it's going to really accelerate the rate at which we can grow our international business.

What's been your experience in international e-commerce?

I tell you what, I just don't think there's a better opportunity available to people. From the time I was a kid, I knew if you can sell a product or service on a local scale, that's great. But if you can get it to a national scale, now you're able to really hit some big numbers. But if you're able to take a product, a service, an idea and implement it on a worldwide, global scale, now the sky is the limit.

How do you present the site so that it reaches these international customers?

Biggest thing on that, honestly, is networking. You want to use your social media to expand. For example, one of our core markets for our product is U.S. diplomatic staff that are stationed overseas. We've got a ton of U.S. diplomatic staff, security personnel, military, that kind of stuff. Well, the Foreign Service people have a forum on Yahoo! where they tell each other—"Oh man, I found this StrongVPN service, it's wonderful—I'm able to surf, now, in the U.S. and know that my traffic is secure." And then someone else writes and says, "Boy, but I found this company, Sabai Technology; they can take that and give it to your whole home instead of just one computer."

By developing social media and by encouraging customers to talk about their experience with you and their friends, and whether your shipping service is good . . . where you can provide an excellent experience, then people are going to talk about you. In providing links, in providing good email support so that they have their tracking number, things like that, you create a customer experience where people want to talk about you. And they're going to talk about you on Facebook, they're going to talk about you on LinkedIn, they're going to talk about you in Yahoo! Groups.

The other strategy is getting on other websites—probably a third of our traffic right now comes from one of our partner companies. By partnering with a company who's already strong and already has a large amount of Web traffic, when they put our company on their site, all of a sudden your traffic just kind of goes through the roof.

What's the most important lesson in exporting?

I would say the number one lesson I've learned is just how critical and crucial customer contact, customer communication, and customer service is. With all the customers that we've had in the Middle East, for example, it's amazing how many times we've heard that this was the best service they've ever gotten. And that's what creates word of mouth; that's what creates loyalty; that's what creates raving fans. And honestly, that is marketing. That will beat traditional print marketing kind of stuff all day long.

And what you've got to do is make sure that front to back, from the time they place an order to the time they get it in their hands—and even after for technical support—that it's seamless; that it's well communicated; that they have a certainty that when they've given you their money, they're going to get their product; that they're able to track it through the process. To me, that's the most important thing for doing successful international business.

And I tell you what's funny in terms of competition: you know you're always going to have competition, you're always going to have people nipping at your heels; but the one place where you can generally compete best is in customer service and in quality of execution. Generally, if someone's going to try to take your business and snag your ideas and compete with your kind of stuff, a lot of times they're going to be looking for the easy money. And customer support ain't easy. Shipping something in 3 days to Dubai ain't easy, you know. You've got to pay for it; you've got to provide that level of service. ⊘

Chris Stock
Sales Manager, Zeigler Brothers

Tell us about the business and what you produce.

We're a manufacturer of specialty animal feeds. We do a variety of feeds. Our focus is aquaculture feeds, specifically for fish and shrimp farms. We also do feeds for pet exotic animals. And we're also involved with the biomedical research industry, helping provide specialty diets for the animals that serve as health models in research.

You're not a Zeigler brother. What's your position with the company?

I manage the sales of the company in Asia. But I strictly focus on the aquaculture area, which is where a lot of our attention and efforts are involved. I'm only involved with export; I don't do any domestic business. My eyes are overseas.

How long have you been exporting?

Zeigler's has been exporting for quite a while. It's very ingrained in the company culture, which is a great reason for our success. In the mid-1980s is probably about the time it started. And our involvement with the aquaculture industry really helped pull us and propel us into export, because aquaculture is a very international business, and it happens more outside the U.S. than inside the U.S.

What's the biggest challenge the company has faced?

We've had quite a few. Zeigler is no stranger to challenges and, fortunately, it's very good at overcoming them. We deal with export challenges all the time. There's a downside to exporting and that is overcoming hurdles and being prepared for them. But we deal with issues such as diseases that affect the crops or with the fish or shrimp we're helping raise. We also had a fire about 5 years ago that devastated one of our production facilities. And through it all, Zeigler has managed to grow and expand. So it's a real testament to the management and to their abilities. There's always something lurking around the next corner.

In recovering from the fire, how did you bounce back?

I think that the management team and the production team were very efficient and organized. And they had a plan and saw it through. It allowed us, I think, to become more efficient, to make the most of what we have, and to modernize some things as well.

We made the most out of what was a terrible situation and really didn't skip a beat. Our customers are very loyal; we're very fortunate to have a great customer base. And they helped see us through. It's amazing how far the company has come since that fire not so long ago.

Tell us about the extent of your exports and how they contribute to the company's success.

Exports have expanded rapidly, especially in the last handful of years. They now encompass a majority of our business—slightly over 50 percent. We're exporting to between 40 and 50 different countries every year. Last count was 43; some come and go. But it's a huge part of our business and it's where we see the most growth opportunity. If we want to grow our business, it's going to be through overseas markets. We certainly have business in the U.S. and that's important to us, but the U.S. market won't be growing at the rate that the international markets will.

> *"If we want to grow our business, it's going to be through overseas markets."*

What markets are you focusing on, going forward?

Areas of specific interest are Africa and Southeast Asia. There are a number of countries in these areas: West Africa is a hotspot for us—specifically Ghana and Nigeria and—and then in Southeast Asia, we look at Bangladesh, China, India, Indonesia, the Philippines, Thailand, and Vietnam.

Chris Stock with customers in Vietnam.

Some people might say: "Africa, it's so risky there." What is attractive to you about Africa?

Africa is on the cusp. Not a lot of people see the opportunity, so it's a great time to get in early because it's a huge emerging middle class that's developing there with spending power. They need things more than any other part of the world. They have a lack of access to some of the higher tech products and things that the U.S. can offer.

And there's reason to take it slow when entering Africa and be cautious, but the opportunity outweighs the risk, there's no doubt about that. As long as you proceed with caution and support from people who have experience there, it's a market companies need to entertain. You can get on the bus early, or you can get on late. The opportunities are there now to get involved.

In meeting all the other companies recently at the President's Export Award ceremony, was there something that struck you as particularly interesting about their profiles?

I think this is a general can-do attitude. I think it's part of who Zeigler is, and I sense it among all the people attending. It's an attitude that we're going to pursue these markets, there are opportunities there, and don't let the problems or the delays hold me back. People are going to go for it and they're going to look past the challenges to the opportunities beyond that. I think you could just sense that attitude amongst the people we spoke to. I mean, that's what it takes to succeed in export. You're not going to do it if you give up at the first challenge. You have to have the long-term vision and the tenacity to pursue it.

> "Africa is on the cusp. Not a lot of people see the opportunity, so it's a great time to get in early because it's a huge emerging middle class that's developing there with spending power."

Do you have an actual plan for growing exports?

Zeigler has medium-long-term plans. And export is a cornerstone to it. Exporting will probably only become more important.

Is it a big plan, a fat plan?

For a small business like Zeigler, I would say so. I think the goals are considerable and we've come so far that it makes the bar we're reaching for a little more realistic. When you look back and see what's been accomplished, you realize that some of the goals you think were far-reaching are maybe more feasible than you thought at first pass.

And do you think that Zeigler is a better company because of exporting, and if so, in what ways?

Absolutely. It diversifies the company, allows us to be insulated from issues in one market or another. Our business is subject to seasonality as well, and it has reduced the impact of seasonality on our manufacturing. And it just connects us throughout the world. The Zeigler brand is known in our industry throughout the world, and that's a tremendous privilege.

And it challenges us. We are able to take opportunities and things we learn in one country and apply them elsewhere. So we're always learning. One of the great parts about our job is we're connecting people throughout the world and bringing ideas from one place to the other, whether or not they directly impact our product. We're a facilitator and our customers see that. And I think it's a very strong point when they get to know us, to see that we're connected throughout the world and bringing solutions from one corner to the next.

Can you think of one example of the learning that took place in one of your international markets that you were able to bring back and do something with?

I'm sure there are many. Offhand, I think one of the things we're more recently learning in the marketing area would be making our products easier to use. In Southeast Asia, we were struggling with language barriers. We've been very ingrained in Latin America, very comfortable working with bilingual Spanish products and clients. But as we enter the Southeast Asian market, we encounter the diversity of languages. Also, because we're in agriculture, one of the end users of our products may have limited education or ability to read—so because our products can be technical in nature, how do we overcome those hurdles? So we've begun developing and incorporating visual aids, videos, icons, logos, things that will help them understand how to use the product and what it's designated for. And we're able to take that and apply it elsewhere, because it is a universal need, but it's being driven by a specific market area force at the moment.

Chris Stock with customers in Armenia.

What has the U.S. government done for you?

The U.S. Commercial Service is kind of a go-to for us when we run into issues. There's always something popping up. When you export to 40 to 50 countries a year, there's going to be something at any given point on your plate. And so it's a common go-to kind of hub for us. For example, in Bangladesh, we were having issues with financing. I needed to verify that the finance rules we were being told about by our client were legitimate; that these were the terms we need to work under. The U.S. Commercial Service was able to connect us with trustworthy local authorities, who could verify this was the case, and we could move on. But in general, we come to them when we have export regulatory issues and we need somebody inside the government to guide us. That's a big thing about exporting: knowing that you don't know it all and you're always going to need support.

The government has helped bring us into new markets. We went on a trade mission to Ghana when we were getting our Africa business warmed up and met people there that are clients now and important partners.

Advice for other U.S. exporters or for companies considering it?

It's a no-brainer. You should be exporting. If you're not, start learning about it, talk to other exporters, and just go for it. I think the key things to exporting are persistence and patience.

You have to realize that when you get in this, it may not be immediate sales, it may take years, but you have to have the long-term vision. If you're willing to go through a couple of ups and downs, it can pay off in dividends. If you don't enter the export market, you're limiting your sales in a big way, no doubt about it. ⊘

Avrum Saunders
Lightning Eliminators

Your company name reminds me of "Ghostbusters." Why do we need to eliminate lightning and how do you do it?

We build very specialized and unique equipment to protect sensitive facilities from lightning strikes. If you have an oil facility, for example, a lightning strike can be catastrophic. Ours is a very different technology than the traditional lightning rod. We avoid lightning strikes, whereas lightning rods attract it.

Can you tell us a bit about how the technology works?

Our technology is designed around a principle called charge transfer. Basically, lightning forms in the following way: Energy forms from the ground up and from the clouds down. And where the two meet, you'll see the lightning strike or the lightning flash. Our equipment is designed to keep that upward-forming energy from reaching sufficient strength to attract the downward energy. It will seek some other location to connect. We are in currently about 70 countries. We have over 3,000 installations around the world. We have a who's who of clients from all the major oil companies, to major industrial firms, and so on.

What percentage of your sales is export?

Sixty-plus percent. I think this year it'll probably reach about 62 to 63 percent. And we've grown that 200 percent over the last 3 1/2 years.

What's caused this growth?

We've taken a different approach to the business. We're not commodity salespeople. We want to work with our clients to figure out what their need is and their risk tolerance, build around their business model, and then design a system that will meet those requirements to protect their facilities. One of the interesting things in the economic downturn is that many companies squeezed out the excess capacity in their systems, whether it be extra factory facilities or whatever, and have realized that they now have to protect against more issues because they can't afford any downtime. So their risk tolerance has gone down dramatically; we've benefited.

The idea is that if you have, let's say, an oil and gas facility. It's a billion-dollar facility. Frankly, do you want to attract lightning to that facility? It sounds like a silly question, but in the traditional mode, that's exactly what they've been doing for all these years, 350 years since Ben Franklin did the kite and key experiment. Our system is designed to have that lightning strike somewhere else.

How serious a problem are lightning strikes in the oil industry?

About 60 percent of our business is oil and gas. But any facility that has electronics is sensitive to lightning strikes. It's a bigger and bigger problem because we're seeing more and more lightning in various places around the world. If you looked at the news over the last few days, you saw the weather patterns in the U.S. are some of the most intense, if not the most intense, in the world and so more and more companies are becoming concerned about lightning and related issues. Most of the reason that we've been successful overseas is because they are much more aware of, and sensitive to, lightning in places like Nigeria, Singapore, the Far East in general, India—the continent of Africa in general. But lightning patterns and weather patterns are changing and, as a consequence, we're seeing lightning in places that we hadn't really seen it before.

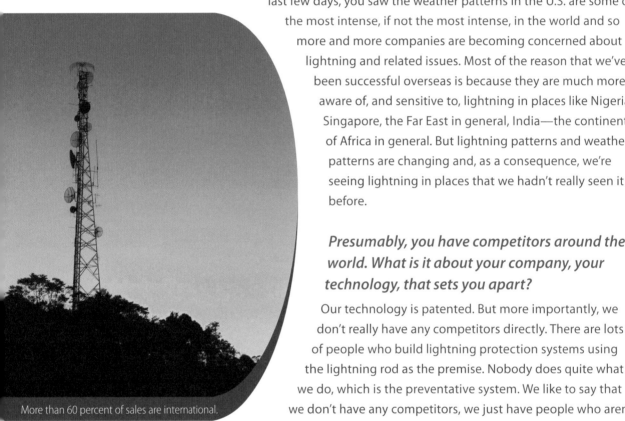
More than 60 percent of sales are international.

Presumably, you have competitors around the world. What is it about your company, your technology, that sets you apart?

Our technology is patented. But more importantly, we don't really have any competitors directly. There are lots of people who build lightning protection systems using the lightning rod as the premise. Nobody does quite what we do, which is the preventative system. We like to say that we don't have any competitors, we just have people who aren't aware of us yet.

How helpful is the U.S. government in helping your international business grow?

Extraordinarily helpful. The people at the U.S. Commercial Service in Denver have been extraordinarily helpful to us. They have helped us open five or six new markets in the last 2 years. In fact, my international sales manager is in Australia as we speak, on a trip organized by the International Trade Administration, working with a local staff member in Australia to introduce our technology more fully and to help us find representation. That's been the single most important thing that they've helped us do: find good representation in a number of different countries. I highly recommend it to anybody who is looking to export. They're good folk.

You have no hang ups working with the government then?

Absolutely not. In fact, the services they provide you could not obtain for 20 to 30 times what it costs us to work with them. It's one of the programs that most people don't know about, unfortunately, but is a really good use of our tax dollars because, for every dollar spent, we're returning a considerably higher sum to the economy in Colorado and the U.S.

Did you have a major challenge in the international area that you were able to overcome?

When you're dealing overseas, and particularly in some of the places that we go, like Nigeria, there are a lot of cultural and legal issues, not the least of which is the Foreign Corrupt Practices Act, which you have to really understand or you can get sideways quickly. Finance is another area that you really have to pay attention to. Those are the two primary things that we've been able, over the last several years, to overcome significantly: understand what the requirements are and, if we don't, know which questions to ask. But we've also received help from the Department of Commerce and others in terms of understanding issues and figuring out solutions. It's been a very good partnership.

The oil industry is a major client.

Do you consider the company better as a result of the exporting?

Absolutely. Dealing domestically is pretty much the same across the country. We are a pretty homogeneous economy. But when you go overseas, you're dealing with very different economies and very different cultures in many places. You have to learn to listen.

That has been one of the great lessons we've learned. And it's helped us overall. Our people are much better at listening to what isn't said as much as what is said. That's the tricky part. You've got to figure out what isn't being said.

Do you recall a particular incident that illustrates the importance of listening?

In the last 2 years, we have done a significant amount of business in the United Arab Emirates. Now, when you first look at UAE, lightning isn't a particularly intense issue. So the question then is, Why are they interested in our equipment? And that's where you have to start listening. What we discovered very quickly is that, because they have the money, they want to protect their people, so they made a business decision to buy our equipment. They are going above and beyond the basics. To sell to a group like that, you have to understand what their business needs are. We've done several millions of dollars' worth of business in the United Arab Emirates.

So they're setting up these systems to prevent something that's a potential in the future but is not a particular problem now?

There's always a problem because it only takes one strike. But they have made the business judgment that they don't want to take that chance. Their risk tolerance is exceedingly low. So they said, "OK, let's spend above and beyond what we might otherwise normally have done to protect our facilities and our people." That was true in the United Arab Emirates and it's true in Singapore and a number of other places. They've gone above and beyond the norm.

U.S. technology and business values are highly regarded.

Set aside the question of global warming—the weather patterns themselves are changing. For example, Japan used to see the strongest lightning in the world. Now, in the northern Atlantic near the Scandinavian countries, we're seeing as intense and sometimes more intense lightning. And it's moving south.

We're beginning to see people ask the following questions: What does that mean for Europe? What do we need to do to protect against tomorrow today because, if you wait until tomorrow and you have a strike, you're in deep trouble.

And that's where the listening comes in.

Exactly. You've got to understand people's business challenges, needs, and models. Once you do that, then you have a conversation to figure out how you can help. But if you're not listening, you're going to miss it.

Advice to the companies that aren't exporting now?

There are three areas that I think are crucial. First, you need quality representation in the local economies because you cannot, from the U.S., fully comprehend what goes on day-to-day in a place like Nigeria. You just can't do it. You need that local help. Secondly, you have to pay attention to the details, such as financing instruments, letters of credit and bank transfers, and things of that sort. Thirdly, and perhaps most importantly, you have to understand the business culture. There are things that we are constrained by, such as the Foreign Corrupt Practices Act. This is very important to understand in places like

"The people at the U.S. Commercial Service in Denver . . . have helped us open five or six new markets in the last two years . . .

Nigeria where there are cultural differences that would run afoul of that law. You have to understand what's going on and you have to address those from the outset because otherwise you can get sucked into some very ugly situations.

Do the other advantages that U.S. companies may have, such as the quality of the technology, the business culture known for its honesty, straightforwardness, and excellent customer service—does that ever trump the $500 or the $5,000 under the table that competitors from other countries might provide?

I will say two things. One is that we have set our ethical standard not to play that game. But, secondly, foreign buyers really do appreciate American technology and quality. We're doing some projects in Nigeria where they insist on buying American because they've been burned by other companies of other nationalities. They just don't want to risk that. And so we do have that advantage. Made in America, overseas, really does have some legs. But you can't do it in an arrogant way. You have to do it in a way that supports their business models. ∅

Leslie Smith

HERO Florida

How did you get started in exporting?

My son and I went to Export 101 at the local university. It was put on by Jacksonville (Florida) Port Authority, the chamber of commerce, and the Department of Commerce. We went to a 6-week course and were the first graduates. We're their friends. We're their little poster child. I think we're their most successful grads up to this point.

I had been in the commercial landscape business for 30 years. We took the knowledge from the course and applied it to mining equipment, which is what we were interested in reselling. So we went to Las Vegas to the big mining show that happens every 4 years.

We decided to have a reception and invited all the commercial specialists from our embassies who were there with delegates from their countries. The delegates are buyers representing mining companies from around the world. And, to our surprise, 200 to 300 showed up, so it was really nice. We made a deal with an outfit in Ghana and sold some equipment. So that's how we got started in the African market.

From there, we hired two country managers. What I mean by country managers is people that are local, that know the area, that know the buyers, and would go around to the mines and ask if they needed things and such. At that point, we kept getting on airplanes.

Why did you decide to go to the export course in the first place? You had a good business.

I just thought it was interesting. I read about it in a business journal and called my son into the office. "Carlton, this course on exporting, it looks interesting." I always wanted to do something like that. I just thought it would be an opportunity to travel and spend time with my son, who is also my business partner.

How many countries are you in now?

We're in a bunch. I think probably 10, including Ghana, Nigeria on the west side, and then lots of southern Africa: Botswana, Zambia, Tanzania, and Namibia. Gosh, lots in that region.

What niche do you occupy?

It's heavy equipment for the mining industry and spare parts, rebuilt motors, and transmissions. We are a reseller.

Were you concerned about the risks of doing business in some parts of Africa?

Yeah, we really were. When we started we could do nothing more than cash and carry. People are not going to be able to open letters of credit and so forth, so it has to be cash and carry. And a lot of times they just don't have the cash. As things have progressed, we've received help from the Export-Import Bank of the U.S., and we're able to finance companies that are worth their salt once they're checked out through Ex-Im. So now we're able to give companies terms.

How does the Bank work for small exporters like you?

As a U.S. government agency, their job is to promote U.S. exports, and they try to tip the scale in favor of exports. In the past, everything was going one way. It's all import instead of exports.

How does the credit program work?

For a company over there, they provide an international credit report and a couple of references, one of which needs to be a U.S. reference. Once approved, they can get an unlimited amount of credit to begin with, and on parts up to 6 months, and for machinery up to 1 year. We don't let our customers get too stretched out. A hundred thousand dollars to $150,000 is the most that we like to do for any one company for any one sale.

> "You have to be willing to go to those places and understand those people so that they trust you and you trust them."

In addition to Ex-Im Bank, did you get help from other government agencies and programs?

The U.S. Commercial Service and the State of Florida through Enterprise Florida—those guys are great. They're constantly bringing people to our office, trying to marry us with other people, inviting us to go on trade missions, and really doing their job. If you've got a question, that's where the support from the Commerce Department really comes in. And I would advise anyone that decides to get into the exporting business to use those resources because that's what they're there for.

> ". . . it's the American dream. It's the entrepreneurial spirit. You go out there and you get it."

So one aspect of the help you received was the International Buyer Program show in Las Vegas?

It's the Mine Expo, which only happens once every 4 years. It's the biggest in the world. The U.S. Commercial Service brings buyer delegations from many different countries with mining equipment needs. In 2008, they had brought delegations from . . . I mean, you name the country, they were there. We didn't have any marketing strategy at that time, but my son thought it would be a good idea to have that reception. And as it turns out, he was right. Man, I'll tell you, there was a bunch of beer drinking at that reception, and whatever cultural differences there were vanished on the spot.

And an immediate sale followed with Ghana without you having to first go there and engage in tedious negotiations?

It did.

How'd that happen?

The drinking. I'm just kidding. This is what we're here for. We're heavy equipment resources. We're a distributor, a sourcing company. Before the Mine Expo, I'd spend a lot of time going to different U.S. manufacturers and saying, "Hey, guys, listen. I'm going to bring more salespeople on but I've got to have the best prices. I've got to have my stuff first."

So I had lists and lists. I knew what type of mining equipment the people who were going to be at the trade show in Vegas had used. I had the equipment at the right price, and I was at the right place with a room full of buyers drinking my beer.

And have you learned things in doing business abroad that have helped make the company more successful?

I think one of the biggest things is the cultural gap. I'm 50. My son and other colleagues are 26. So I come from an era when you could remember a hundred phone numbers—when you had a beeper and stuff. So face-to-face is very important to me. Well, now you've got the Internet, and you think, "Why would anybody use my company?" That's where the face-to-face comes in. It's very important. People have to trust me and I have to trust them. That's what I think I've learned: If you're going to export, you have to be willing to get on that plane. You have to be willing to go to those places and understand those people so that they trust you and you trust them. And then you've got to do it again on the U.S. side, and get people to trust you. When we say we're going to do something, we do it. It's as simple as that.

You've had a great time traveling back and forth, haven't you?

We've had a wonderful time. It's a way for me to keep my young man with me. At 26, he has to travel with me. Not many fathers get that opportunity.

And you've met some amazing people.

Very interesting and wonderful characters. We've had crazy drivers that ran over the village goat, driving 200 miles an hour. I got sick one time in Tarkwa and they thought that I had malaria, which I didn't. They brought me to the hospital in Tarkwa, which is outside of the capital city of Accra in Ghana.

> "I had the equipment at the right price, and I was at the right place with a room full of buyers drinking my beer."

We got to the hospital and the gates are locked. The hospital is closed. So they bring me to a healer. They think I'm dying. So we get there. The drums are beating, people are dancing around. They lay me on this bamboo thing like they were smoking fish. Then this lady, I think her name was Miss Rudolph, comes out with her face painted, and starts examining me.

She's got me by the back of the head and hits me with a shooter of fish soup. And the next thing I know, I woke up around 3 o'clock in the morning. Carlton is sitting over me. He's rubbing my head with a wet rag. When he sees me wake up, he yells, "Dad's back!"

When traveling, you should try to take good care of yourself and make sure that when you or your spouse pack your ditty bag, you've got plenty of medicines and antibiotics. If you get somewhere you can get in trouble.

What advice do you have for companies that aren't exporting now?

It's not for everybody. You've got to be willing to be away from home. You've got to be willing to not have some of the comforts that you have at home. You've got to be willing to sit on a plane for many hours at a time.

But it's the American dream. It's the entrepreneurial spirit. You go out there and you get it. I've always been in my own business, so it's a lot of fun. I think my son thinks the same way, and his friends. If you want to travel and you want to do something exciting, take as many classes and talk to as many people like me as you can before you jump off the cliff. Otherwise, you could spend a lot of money and not go anywhere. Do your homework. Use all the resources that the Commerce Department has to offer, because they have a lot. Start out slow and go on some of these (Commerce Department or state government) trade missions and do it like that. And number one, have a good product—one that sells. ⌀

Attila Szucs
Advanced Superabrasives, Inc.

Your namesake was known for pillaging and plundering. Have you adopted some of his techniques in order to succeed in international business?

Hungarians are very proud of their history and their heroes. The Attila of whom you speak was the Hun in Hungary. After World War II, part of Hungary became Romania. Many Hungarian parents named their children after him. That's how I ended up Attila the Romanian and now the American.

You seem mild-mannered.

I'll let others be the judge of my character. I suppose I could have been named Genghis Khan.

Tell us about your company.

The company was founded in 1993 in Nashville, North Carolina. We started with myself and another person, and today we're exporting to 16 countries around the world.

What do you produce?

We manufacture superabrasive grinding wheels for other manufacturers.

What is a superabrasive grinding wheel?

It is a product that actually grinds hard materials such as ceramic, glass, quartz, and steel—all materials that need to be manufactured to very high tolerances. And the best way to do that is through grinding.

How did you come to create this company?

As I mentioned, I was born in Romania. My father and the entire family emigrated from Romania in 1973 to the U.S. We settled in New Jersey. That's where I went to school. I used to work for a company in New Jersey that was manufacturing diamond grinding wheels. In 1993, I decided to branch out on my own and start Advanced Superabrasives.

I decided to move down to the western part of North Carolina because I really liked the climate and the mountains.

How did you get the entrepreneur bug? Was it from your father or other experiences?

It was from my father. He had his own business. He started his own business in the U.S. not too long after we arrived here. And he is the entrepreneur in the family, and that's where I got it from.

What was the biggest challenge that you faced in the development of your company?

We started with absolutely no sales in 1993, and we did a lot of research and development and testing to improve our product. Slowly but surely we started penetrating the market within the U.S. We started exporting in 1995 to Canada. Around 2002, when the economy took a hit in the U.S., we started to look at how we could diversify so we could insulate ourselves from the economic downturn. That's when we decided to look at exports, and we started exporting to China and to Brazil.

> "Most small U.S. companies don't know about the tremendous asset that we have, whether it's from the federal or the state [government]."

Difficult places to export to.

Very. Brazil's duties and taxes are very high. Make sure you have a good and candid relationship with your buyer. Let them deal with customs issue. In comparison, China's duties and taxes are lower, but still more than what the U.S. charges. The issue in China is IP protection. We prevent reverse engineering of our product by mixing up some of the chemical components, which makes it very hard to copy. The second thing we do is perform the final assembly in Hong Kong. By law, Hong Kong requires that 30 percent of the value of products be assembled there in order to be considered as made in Hong Kong. So we send things we make in North Carolina to Hong Kong for final assembly. That's another way we protect our IP and gain access to the mainland market. Still, it can be tough going. The Chinese make grinding machines for 10 percent of our price.

How did you manage?

We were lucky. We started talking to the U.S. Commercial Service, from Charlotte, North Carolina. It was just wonderful how we were treated and how much of a help they were. Through their Gold Key program (which helps to find buyers), we got into Brazil. And that program is so helpful—they set everything up for us and basically all we had to do was show up. They even helped us with an interpreter and set up all the appointments. It was a wonderful experience. From that point on, we really tried to work very closely with the U.S. Department of Commerce. And we also had the North Carolina Department of Commerce, who were also very helpful in navigating us through the exporting issues that have come up.

But how did you know to contact these people to begin with? You've mentioned just showing up. That's something that a lot of U.S. companies fail to do.

Most small U.S. companies don't know about the tremendous asset that we have, whether it's from the federal or the state level. We first heard about the U.S. Department of Commerce from another company, which helped them export. That's why we contacted them, because we wanted to see how we could pursue the same route.

It was word of mouth.

Yes, it was. And I wish more companies would know about it.

Tell them.

We do. As a matter of fact, in Asheville we started an international show called Grind Tech USA. We have companies from all over the world come to Asheville to display their products. We invite a speaker from the U.S. Department of Commerce because we want to spread the word to other U.S. companies about just great of an entity U.S. Department of Commerce is.

Thank you for doing that. Have you learned things in your dealing with other countries—China, Brazil, elsewhere—that have made you a better company?

We just came back from Seoul, Korea. We participated in Trade Winds Asia. It is a tremendous amount of help to any U.S. company, especially small companies like ours, because we get to meet companies from the region—potential customers, potential distributors. Plus, we learn about the culture of each country in the region and what they're looking for, so we can better prepare ourselves when we start dealing with these companies. It was invaluable for us.

Taking this information, have you modified your product at all, or modified your approach to doing business as a result of what you've learned by selling to people in other cultures?

We absolutely had to, because different cultures have different needs and we really have to cater to their needs. We can't use the same approach in Europe that we're using in Asia. And being from Europe, I actually have a harder time selling in Europe, which is a little bit funny but it's definitely true. The U.S. does have a good following. People around the world, especially in Asia, look up to the U.S. and to U.S. products. So if you're sincere and you have a good product, you have a very good chance of selling overseas, especially in Asia.

And you have a good product, but it's not the only product out there. What would you describe as your "secret sauce" that has made your company successful?

One of the things we do that's different from our competitors is we don't just sell a product. We actually qualify the customer. We ask an awful lot of questions, and custom-design the product to their needs. There is no reason to sell a high-end product to a manufacturing facility that does not have the high-end equipment. That's why we try to tailor-make each product to each manufacturer. On top of that, if there is a need, we send some of our sales engineers to coach the people and help them grind and make the product work for them.

So the bigger companies really can't afford, or it's not in their interests, to do this customization?

The larger companies, they like to sell their catalog. They have off-the-shelf products. They do not customize like we do. And customizing is a lot more difficult, so for a large company it's really not worth it because the sales are not there. For us, that's a niche market. And we go in; we help the customer. We make them a lot more efficient.

You have to be very good at listening, don't you?

Very good at listening. We have to know a lot of different machines. We have to know not just about the grinding wheel itself but about the machinery and everything that's related to our grinding wheel.

Are you confident that, after your recent trip to Asia, you'll add to your current collection of country markets?

Yes, I'm looking forward to adding Korea and Japan. Japan is the crown jewel for me.

Will the free-trade agreement with Korea help?

I think it will. Anytime we have a free-trade agreement, it definitely helps. And it removes some of the obstacles.

> *"So if you're sincere and you have a good product, you have a very good chance of selling overseas, especially in Asia.*

What's your advice to U.S. companies that aren't exporting now?

You don't have to be a large company to export. That's number one. We're a prime example. We're not a large company. Second, take one country at a time. Finally, and most importantly, get help. I would highly recommend using the U.S. Department of Commerce and your own local state department of commerce, because it will help navigate those troubled waters of export. Depending on which country you're trying to get into, it could be a tremendous help to have people help you with the exports.

I'm thankful that I'm in this country and had the opportunity to get to where I am today. I always tell the people from the U.S. Department of Commerce and the North Carolina Department of Commerce what a great job they do. And I think if more small companies would know about it, our country would benefit tremendously because we could export more instead of importing. ⌀

The CS
Global Network

About the U.S. Commercial Service

The U.S. Commercial Service (CS) is the export promotion arm of the U.S. Department of Commerce's International Trade Administration. Our global network of more than 1,400 trade professionals is located throughout the United States and in U.S. embassies and consulates in more than 70 countries. Whether you're looking to make your first international sale or expand to additional markets, we offer support, knowledge, and lucrative opportunities to increase your bottom line.

For more information on how CS can help your business increase its international sales, please contact one of our local offices or visit *export.gov/industry*.

U.S. Offices

Alabama
Birmingham

Alaska
Anchorage

Arizona
Phoenix
Scottsdale
Tucson

Arkansas
Little Rock
Rogers

California
Bakersfield
Cabazon
Fresno
Inland Empire
Los Angeles (Downtown)
Los Angeles (West)
Newport Beach
North Bay
Oakland
Sacramento
San Diego
San Francisco
San Jose
Ventura County

Colorado
Denver

Connecticut
Middletown

Delaware
Served by Philadelphia, PA

District of Columbia
Served by Arlington, VA

Florida
Clearwater
Fort Lauderdale
Jacksonville
Miami
Orlando
Tallahassee

Georgia
Atlanta
Savannah

Hawaii
Honolulu

Idaho
Boise

Illinois
Chicago
Libertyville
Peoria
Rockford

Indiana
Indianapolis

Iowa
Des Moines

Kansas
Wichita

Kentucky
Lexington
Louisville

Louisiana
New Orleans
Shreveport

Maine
Portland

Maryland
Baltimore

Massachusetts
Boston

Michigan
Detroit
Grand Rapids
Pontiac
Ypsilanti

Minnesota
Minneapolis

Mississippi
Jackson

Missouri
Kansas City
St. Louis

Montana
Missoula

Nebraska
Omaha

Nevada
Las Vegas
Reno

New Hampshire
Portsmouth

New Jersey
Newark
Trenton

New Mexico
Santa Fe

New York
Buffalo
Harlem
Long Island
New York
Rochester
Westchester

North Carolina
Charlotte
Greensboro
Raleigh

North Dakota
Fargo

Ohio
Akron
Cincinnati
Cleveland
Columbus
Toledo

Oklahoma
Oklahoma City
Tulsa

Oregon
Portland

Pennsylvania
Harrisburg
Philadelphia
Pittsburgh

Puerto Rico
San Juan

Rhode Island
Providence

South Carolina
Charleston
Columbia
Greenville

South Dakota
Sioux Falls

Tennessee
Knoxville
Memphis
Nashville

Texas
Austin
El Paso
Fort Worth
Grapevine
Houston
McAllen
Midland
San Antonio

Utah
Salt Lake City

Vermont
Montpelier

Virginia
Arlington
Richmond

Washington
Seattle
Spokane

West Virginia
Charleston
Wheeling

Wisconsin
Milwaukee

Wyoming
Served by Denver, CO

International Offices

Afghanistan
Kabul

Algeria
Algiers

Argentina
Buenos Aires

Australia
Perth
Sydney

Austria
Vienna

Belgium
Brussels

Brazil
Belo Horizonte
Brasília
Recife
Rio de Janeiro
São Paulo

Bulgaria
Sofia

Canada
Calgary
Montreal
Ottawa
Toronto

Chile
Santiago

China
Beijing
Chengdu
Guangzhou
Shanghai
Shenyang

Colombia
Bogotá

Costa Rica
San José

Croatia
Zagreb

Czech Republic
Prague

Denmark
Copenhagen

Dominican Republic
Santo Domingo

Egypt
Cairo

El Salvador
San Salvador

European Union
Brussels

Finland
Helsinki

France
Paris

Germany
Berlin
Düsseldorf
Frankfurt
Munich

Ghana
Accra

Greece
Athens

Guatemala
Guatemala City

Honduras
Tegucigalpa

Hong Kong

Hungary
Budapest

India
Ahmedabad
Bangalore
Chennai
Hyderabad
Kolkata
Mumbai
New Delhi

Indonesia
Jakarta

Iraq
Baghdad

Ireland
Dublin

Israel
Tel Aviv

Italy
Milan
Rome

Japan
Osaka-Kobe
Tokyo

Jordan
Amman

Kazakhstan
Almaty

Kenya
Nairobi

Korea (South)
Seoul

Kuwait
Kuwait City

Lebanon
Beirut

Libya
Tripoli

Malaysia
Kuala Lumpur

Mexico
Guadalajara
Mexico City
Monterrey

Morocco
Casablanca

Netherlands
The Hague

New Zealand
Wellington

Nigeria
Lagos

Norway
Oslo

Pakistan
Islamabad
Karachi
Lahore

Panama
Panama City

Peru
Lima

Philippines
Manila

Poland
Warsaw

Portugal
Lisbon

Qatar
Doha

Romania
Bucharest

Russia
Moscow
St. Petersburg

Saudi Arabia
Dhahran
Jeddah
Riyadh

Serbia
Belgrade

Singapore

Slovak Republic
Bratislava

South Africa
Cape Town
Johannesburg

Spain
Madrid

Sweden
Stockholm

Taiwan
Kaohsiung
Taipei

Thailand
Bangkok

Turkey
Ankara
Istanbul
Izmir

Ukraine
Kiev

United Arab Emirates
Abu Dhabi
Dubai

United Kingdom
London

Uruguay
Montevideo

Vietnam
Hanoi
Ho Chi Minh City

West Bank
Jerusalem